PRAISE FOR
Health Insurance: Navigating Traps and Gaps

"Maura Carley has written an important book for anyone who has to navigate our nation's fractured, fragmented, inadequate health insurance system. Case studies, drawn from years of experience helping individuals and families, provide insight into how these defects can affect us. No one will emerge from reading this book without a deepened understanding of how today's insurance model leaves us vulnerable to tragic medical and economic consequences."
David M. Lawrence
Chairman and CEO (retired)
Kaiser Foundation Health Plan and Kaiser Foundation Hospitals, Inc.
San Francisco Bay Area, California

"Today we are faced with new, convoluted health care laws and ever-changing health insurance plans, eligibility and enrollment rules. Making the best choice is akin to finding the proverbial needle in a haystack. The good news is that help is here—Maura Carley's book, *Health Insurance: Navigating Traps & Gaps*, is a must-read as a reference and to inspire you to take action to protect your family's savings, medical coverage and peace of mind."
Peggy Fleming Jenkins (and husband Greg Jenkins, M.D.)
Olympic Gold Medalist in Figure Skating
San Francisco Bay Area, California

"There is no clearer explanation of how Medicare works than *Health Insurance: Navigating Traps & Gaps* by Maura Carley. Every person going onto Medicare should read it and every person on Medicare should read it. Throughout the years Maura Carley and her colleagues at Healthcare Navigation have always given me and my family terrific advice regarding my choices in health care. In *Health Insurance: Navigating Traps & Gaps* Ms. Carley also explains that in addition to understanding Medicare it is imperative that you understand your retiree medical benefits and how they can change or even be eliminated. Read this book."
Peter Gogolak
Former Professional Football Player
Sales Director, R.R.Donnelley & Sons Co.
Darien, Connecticut

"I have known Maura Carley for years. When I retained her firm, Healthcare Navigation, they handled a burdensome situation with remarkable effectiveness and results. If you need to understand healthcare coverage, read *Health Insurance: Navigating Traps & Gaps*."
Susan Whiting
Media Executive
Chicago, Illinois

"I have built several companies and always made sure that I had excellent healthcare coverage. When I sold my last company, I was faced with a transition to Medicare. This was a traumatic, processing nightmare. Medicare choices used to be simple, but not any more. I received invaluable expert advice and guidance from Maura Carley and her staff at Healthcare Navigation and I recommend that anyone dealing with healthcare decisions especially Medicare, read *Health Insurance: Navigating Traps & Gaps*."
Irene Cohen
Partner, Cohen and Miners
Co-Founder, FlexCorp Systems, LLC
Westport, Connecticut

"My husband and I have been clients of Healthcare Navigation for years. Our primary insurance coverage is through my husband's firm which is based in Bermuda. We were delighted when our financial advisors referred us to a firm that had the expertise to handle foreign claims. Plus, they are always there for us. Their wealth of knowledge is now available in Maura's book *Health Insurance: Navigating Traps & Gaps*. Maura's made a difficult topic extremely reader-friendly and I strongly recommend you read it."
Jean Hamilton Pearman (and husband Richard S.L. Pearman)
Paget, Bermuda

"I was stunned when my wife and I were denied insurance and truly flabbergasted when my infant granddaughter was also denied insurance. Fortunately I was referred to Healthcare Navigation and they resolved our problems. They are the experts. Now Maura Carley has written *Health Insurance: Navigating Traps & Gaps*. If you want to protect your family and learn about our broken healthcare system, read Maura's book."

Mr. Richard F. Timmins (and wife Bonnie Timmins)
Vice President, Finance (retired)
Cisco Systems
Austin, Texas

"When my insurance was abruptly and inexplicably terminated, Maura Carley and her staff overcame every obstacle to get my coverage re-instated. Their work was masterful. If you need guidance, you must read Maura's book, *Health Insurance: Navigating Traps & Gaps*, or better yet, call her."

Nancy J. Brown
Darien, Connecticut and Sarasota, Florida

"Maura Carley and her staff at Healthcare Navigation have taken care of three generations of our family for many years. Knowing we can call for help at any time is invaluable. Now their knowledge and experience is available in *Health Insurance: Navigating Traps & Gaps*. This is an essential book for anyone trying to navigate our healthcare system. Read it."

Mr. and Mrs. Richard G. Woolworth
Lititz, Pennsylvania and Hobe Sound, Florida

"I read about Healthcare Navigation in the *Wall Street Journal*. That was a lucky find. They helped my wife and me with several coverage transitions including relocation. I had no idea the extent to which moving affects your health insurance and the bureaucratic headaches one can face. The next best thing to Healthcare Navigation's skillful support is Maura Carley's book, *Health Insurance: Navigating Traps & Gaps*. I recommend you read it."

Mr. Walter S. Bearden (and wife Noel Bowden Bearden)
Nashville, Tennessee

"Maura Carley and her staff have helped my family with every type of coverage transition—from group to individual coverage, from group to Medicare, and then back to group again. Having skilled professionals to rely on brought us great peace of mind. If you're facing a transition alone, you definitely need Maura's book, *Health Insurance: Navigating Traps & Gaps*."

Pegeen Rubinstein
Corporate Executive
Westport, Connecticut

"Healthcare Navigation was an important part of my support team that helped me with the challenge of recovering from pancreatic cancer. They were there at every step of the way during my illness. I don't know what I would have done without them. I handed-off much of the burden I was dealing with to their skilled staff. If you're going it alone, I highly recommend you read *Health Insurance: Navigating Traps & Gaps*."

Ann Kusumoto
Durham, North Carolina

"Maura Carley's firm, Healthcare Navigation, is an indispensable part of my family's (three generations) life. Now, through her book, *Health Insurance: Navigating Traps & Gaps*, she can also be an indispensable part of yours."

Alexandra Lebenthal
President & CEO
Alexandra and James
New York, New York

"When I retired from my financial advisory firm, my wife and I had ample time to plan our transition onto Medicare which we assumed would be straightforward. After all, I had dealt with complex financial matters on behalf of clients for years and my wife had worked in healthcare. Instead we found ourselves lost in the alphabet soup, acronyms, and terms which dealing with Medicare entails. We received expert guidance from Healthcare Navigation and are delighted that Maura Carley has written a book that can help others manage their transition to Medicare."

Michael L. Stein (and wife Judith Rhinestine)
Principal (retired)
Brownson, Rhemus and Foxworth, Inc.
Chicago, Illinois

"Maura Carley's book, *Health Insurance: Navigating Traps & Gaps* is an indispensable guide to the arcane world of health insurance. The most precious asset anyone has is good health. Biomedical research is accelerating and remarkable new treatments are being developed but without understanding how to maintain proper health insurance, those treatments may be beyond reach. Maura Carley has spent most of her career understanding the complexities, technicalities and irrationalities of health insurance. Her book is full of wisdom that comes from decades of practical experience. Obtaining the right health insurance is critically important and Carley's book is the best source of information on that vital topic."

Leslie D. Michelson
Chairman and Chief Executive Officer
Private Health Management
Los Angeles, California

"Maura Carley's enlightening book, *Health Insurance: Navigating Traps & Gaps*, should be in the horror section of the bookstore. These real-life stories tell the chilling tales of coverage gaps and insurance disputes that kept patients in a perpetual state of pain. As a private Emergency Medicine physician, I want my clients' pain and heartache to heal ASAP. It's troubling to think that medical insurance coverage, or lack of it, can extend this heartache. Maura has helped many of my clients avoid or recover from such events. In *Health Insurance: Navigating Traps & Gaps*, she offers clear and common sense steps that would benefit anyone, particularly in the dynamic time of shifting healthcare policies."

Chris Sidford, M.D.
Founder and Medical Director
Black Bag
Newburyport, Massachusetts

"Maura Carley is one of the most insightful people I know on the subject of understanding the complexity of health insurance. She is the preeminent thought leader on the subject. Carley's book, *Health Insurance: Navigating Traps & Gaps* offers solutions for all who try to understand a system that often defies reason. This book will become a classic for everyone looking to protect themselves and their families. It is a must-read."

Rick Miners
Co-Founder, FlexCorp Systems, LLC
and Author, *Don't Retire, REWIRE!*
New York, New York

HEALTH INSURANCE

Navigating
Traps & Gaps

Maura Loughlin Carley, MPH, CIC

AMP&RSAND, INC.

Chicago • New Orleans

ISBN 978-1-4507-9591-3

Design: David Robson, Robson Design

Published by
AMPERSAND, INC.
1050 North State Street
Chicago, Illinois 60610

203 Finland Place
New Orleans, Louisiana 70131

www.ampersandworks.com

—————

www.healthcarenavigation.com

Printed in U. S. A.

To Jack Carley and Irene Cohen

ACKNOWLEDGMENTS

I could not have written this book without the support of our clients. My colleagues, Bonnie Tuttle, Anne McGuire and Shan Burchenal, were critically important, as always, in identifying key issues and offering ideas. Eileen Carley and Sarah Gravelin researched legislation and facts. My husband, Jack, was an invaluable editor and sounding board.

Finally, Suzie Isaacs' editing and David Robson's design, made the book read and look better than I could have imagined.

CONTENTS

FOREWORD

Most people understand that when dealing with serious illness or injury, they must be concerned about their healthcare coverage. However, many don't appreciate the potentially devastating traps and gaps related to a change in coverage. Less comprehensive or less desirable coverage resulting from any of the following transitions can be devastating:

+ Turning 26 and aging off a parent's Plan
+ Divorce
+ Job loss or job change
+ Retirement or spouse's retirement
+ Moving
+ Company acquisition
+ Death of a spouse

Becoming eligible for Medicare can often improve one's coverage protection. However, Medicare is complex and there are also traps and gaps associated with not handling enrollment properly, or making poor decisions regarding secondary or drug coverage.

I have seen so much heartache, much of which might have been avoided, or at least lessened, had people going through a healthcare coverage transition only been better informed. Americans are often ignorant about health insurance issues because most of us have coverage through a job and don't learn about coverage because our employer is managing the process for us. Everyone with health insurance of any kind needs to be knowledgeable about health insurance matters. Serious illness can be tragic; but not understanding if your coverage will protect you can also be tragic. That is why I wrote this book. I want to share our firm's collective knowledge and experience to help you protect yourself and your family.

My objectives for all readers are as follows:

- Strive to maintain good medical coverage without a gap throughout your entire life
- Know enough about medical insurance to understand how you are or are not protected
- Develop a preliminary "Coverage Plan" that includes steps you will take should you face an abrupt loss of or change in coverage
- Be wary of the dysfunction of our healthcare system

If certain provisions in The Patient Protection and Affordable Care Act of 2010, sometimes referred to as "healthcare reform," "Obamacare," or "ACA" are implemented in 2014, additional coverage options may be provided for many Americans. Those options, however, may not be the best alternative for you or your family. All coverage options should be considered when facing a transition because you should have the best coverage protection possible, consistent with your priorities and values and what you can afford.

Because I mention time and again that healthcare coverage issues are ever-changing, some details in this book may be out-of-date as soon as it's printed. However, the concepts will not go out-of-date. Healthcare coverage is not all the same and never will be. Far from it, coverage is increasingly complex. It's more important than ever to understand these issues because the lack of good healthcare coverage protection can be both financially and emotionally devastating.

Many source materials in the book are actual documents or excerpts from actual documents. This is not meant to criticize any company or organization mentioned. Very simply, facts are compelling. Case Studies are provided throughout to exemplify coverage transition traps and gaps. These are actual client stories. The names have been changed for all but Luci Watson's family who wanted their story told. Although other individuals cannot be identified, their situations are quite real. Many will make you gasp.

Maura Carley
Darien, Connecticut

Clueless about Coverage

O ver the years I have spoken to many people about healthcare concepts and terms and have observed their eyes glaze over even when the matter at hand was of critical importance to them. As a result, before providing the background information you'll need to understand some of the relevant issues, I am presenting five case examples.

Each of the first four case examples is a horrific story illustrating different traps and gaps associated with healthcare coverage transitions. The fifth story is a tragedy of a different sort; a tragedy due to serious illness but important because it illustrates a healthcare coverage situation that was vastly improved by relocating from one state to another and qualifying for superior healthcare coverage as a resident of the new state.

I hope these stories will help you become engaged.

Involuntary Job Loss

Mr. and Mrs. Robert Peters lived in a Connecticut suburb. Mr. Peters was an engineer and Mrs. Peters was a stay-at-home mom raising her children and now helping her children with their children. Mr. Peters' employers had provided good group healthcare coverage throughout their lives. While in his 50s, the firm Mr. Peters worked for had a reduction in force and Mr. Peters lost his position. He thought that with his experience he would be re-employed quickly. Mr. Peters maintained healthcare coverage for himself and his wife by taking COBRA (temporary extension of group coverage) to bridge the transition to a new job and new group coverage. Within months, however, the engineering firm declared bankruptcy and terminated group coverage. Although the individual pays for COBRA coverage, COBRA is always tied to an active employer or union group. When there is no group, there is no COBRA coverage either, so Mr. and Mrs. Peters lost their group coverage.

Given that Mr. Peters had been unemployed for a while, the most affordable insurance option for them was in the private, individual insurance marketplace, which in their state would only be granted based on good health. The couple applied for individual coverage and, fortunately, was accepted. Later, their insurance company, Mutual of Omaha, decided to vacate the individual insurance marketplace in Connecticut, so all individuals covered through the insurer were dropped and had to shop for new coverage. By that time, Mr. Peters had developed serious cardiovascular disease and because of this pre-existing condition could not be approved for coverage in the individual, private insurance marketplace. Mrs. Peters was able to obtain comprehensive coverage because she remained in good health.

At this point since he had also been unemployed for some time, Mr. Peters felt they couldn't afford coverage through the state's high risk pool, Connecticut's Health Reinsurance Association, even though he could qualify for it. After all, based on his age he was in the most expensive category of individuals seeking this coverage. In 2011, the monthly premium for a man in his 60s was $1,829.01.

Mr. Peters could qualify for a very limited benefit Plan through AARP so he bought it thinking some protection was better than none. Mr. Peters' health tragically deteriorated and after a lengthy illness, he died. Even after the AARP policy had paid what it should have, Mr. Peters' rather modest estate still owed a six figure amount to the local hospital, St. Vincent's Medical Center, and owed thousands of dollars to various doctors. We worked with Mrs. Peters and her attorneys on a settlement agreement with the Hospital. In essence, the Hospital discounted its charges and Mrs. Peters agreed to a multi-year payment plan.

The most frightening part of this story is that Mr. and Mrs. Peters did everything right—everything they should have. They were never cavalier or reckless. Nevertheless, they were trapped. Mr. Peters lived in a state where he could have purchased a policy in spite of pre-existing conditions. That insurance coverage was so expensive, however, that it was essentially unavailable to him. Mr. and Mrs. Peters had hoped that his health could hold out until 65 when he would have been eligible for Medicare but that didn't happen. Instead, Mrs. Peters faced years of medical payments that she really could not afford.

Moving Associated with Promotion

Mr. and Mrs. Richard Stevens were employed professionals in their 40s. Mr. Stevens worked for a large furniture retailer; his wife Sharon, worked for a small, local non-profit organization. Through Richard's company they had excellent healthcare coverage from a Preferred Provider Organization with out-of-network benefits.

Mr. Stevens was promoted to a position in a neighboring state but Sharon continued in her job, commuting back and forth. Their new coverage was with a Health Plan in the new state. They experienced a lengthy delay in getting new identification cards and an even longer delay receiving Plan materials. After finally receiving identification cards, Mrs. Stevens arranged time off from work, selected a physician, and had a physical examination. Mrs. Stevens had a questionable mammogram and ultimately breast cancer was diagnosed. Mrs. Stevens had chemotherapy and multiple surgeries in the state where she was working rather than the neighboring state where her husband's new position was located. All her care was denied by the Health Plan. We worked with the Stevens for many months to resolve this lengthy dispute. Not only was information about the Plan not provided timely to the Stevens, once received the information was also extremely confusing. Although the Plan functioned like a Health Maintenance Organization (HMO), a Plan with a limited network, the language in Plan materials was inscrutable. The following excerpt is from one of my appeal letters:

I have read the entire Health Plan Blue Care Certificate of Coverage and find no reference to an HMO. Again, the term "HMO" is not in the 64 page booklet. In fact, the sections on non-participating providers, the Blue Card Program, and the references to out-of-state providers who participate with Blue Cross and Blue Shield Plans, would lead anyone to believe this is an open panel Plan with a gatekeeper.

Even more frightening, the two oncologists (and only two) available to Mrs. Stevens through her HMO had questionable backgrounds. The senior oncologist had surrendered privileges to practice in New York and also surrendered hospital privileges at a local hospital due to charges of professional misconduct associated with narcotics abuse. His junior partner didn't have such an unseemly background but was not even board-eligible in oncology because he had never become board certified in internal medicine. These two were partners and the only participating oncologists in the local Health Plan.

We won the appeal against the Health Plan but it was a long, protracted, laborious battle which ironically would never have happened had Mr. Stevens not been promoted to his new position. The traps in this case were numerous—a delay in benefit materials being forwarded, the materials themselves being terribly misleading with blatantly incorrect information printed on the Plan identification cards, leading anyone to believe they had out-of-network benefits with access to a national network. Even though the employee had no control over any of these issues, the employee's wife was left to fend for herself when care was denied. In this particular situation the employer could have been far more helpful but didn't intervene or assist in any meaningful way.

Exhausting COBRA
and Becoming Uninsured

Early in his career, Stuart Burns held several positions of increasing responsibility in corporate America. In his mid-30s he decided to head out on his own and became a self-employed consultant working for a number of different companies. He also had gone through a divorce and exercised his right to stay on his former wife's Plan through COBRA (temporary extension of group coverage) for three years. Mr. Burns didn't receive any significant healthcare services while on COBRA. When COBRA ended he intended to research his coverage options but he just didn't get to it. As a result, Mr. Burns was uninsured.

One January during a business lunch in New Jersey he had a massive aneurysm and was taken to a local medical center. During his first two months in the hospital, charges from the hospital and all physicians approached $600,000.00. Mr. Burns needed inpatient rehabilitation after hospitalization and a great deal of care after that. Since Mr. Burns did not have insurance at that time, the hospital charges were vastly higher than what insured people normally pay. One's only financial protection in healthcare today is to receive care within a network for which rates have been negotiated. If you are out-of-network or uninsured, you have no financial protection and your provider, hospital, doctor or other, can charge what they choose, reasonable or not.

The hospital and doctors who cared for Mr. Burns saved his life. He was the first to say so. The medical and hospital bills, however, were staggering. It was our job to help broker reasonable settlements. The hospital's original bill to Mr. Burns was over half-a-million dollars. The hospital ultimately discounted its original charges by 75%, accepting $139,000.00. Why would the hospital have initially charged so much? The uninsured are often charged vastly higher rates because they don't have the protection of an insurer and an insurer's network.

Although the hospital agreed to much lower charges, Mr. Burns paid dearly for not obtaining health insurance after his COBRA coverage expired.

Death of a Spouse

On a late afternoon the Friday before a Labor Day weekend, I left work early to play tennis with friends. As I left the court, I met another friend, David Watson, and we talked. I had just dropped off three of our children at college, including our younger daughters, Lisa and Meg, who were just starting their freshman year. David and his wife, Luci, had just dropped off their son, Jamie, who was also starting his freshman year. Our children had known each other since grade school. Older siblings, Eileen Carley and Taylor Watson, were also the same age and friends. David and I talked about our first week as "empty nesters" and David reminded me, "There will be life after children."

The following Sunday afternoon, David suffered a massive coronary while riding his bike in town and died. He left a new widow and two college age children behind. It was an unspeakable loss.

Later that month, another friend, Tricia Daigle, David's insurance broker called me. Until then I hadn't known that David had healthcare coverage as a sole proprietor or self-employed individual. Tricia had been in touch with David's insurer, ConnectiCare, and their position was that David's group of one expired when he died and therefore Luci's and her children's coverage would terminate at the end of the month or in a few days.

Having just experienced the sudden and totally unexpected death of her husband, it was a horrible time to discuss healthcare coverage with Luci but we had to. Tricia and I advised her we should challenge ConnectiCare in order to buy time. After all, even though David had died, the business had to have a wind-down period and our position was that she had stepped in to run the business full time. Nevertheless on October 3, Tricia received a letter shown on page 24 in its entirety but quoted below, retroactively terminating the family's coverage as of September 30.

Letter dated September 30, 2005 and received by broker October 3, 2005

Dear Patricia: I am responding to your question regarding continuation of coverage for the spouse and child of the deceased employee in a *one-life group. Since the decedent was the only employee covered under the group, then the group ceased to exist when he died. COBRA is a continuation of benefits under a group policy that continues in force so COBRA is not available where there is no group policy to continue benefits from… **Termination will be September 30 and October premium will be returned.** Since our group policies have no conversion feature, there is no conversion to an individual Plan available. **I have mailed a ConnectiCare Solo enrollment kit to Luci Watson in case she would like to consider applying.** However, please advise client that it will be medically underwritten and coverage is not guaranteed issue.*

At that point, neither Tricia nor I had dealt with a situation where coverage was terminated so abruptly. There was no opportunity for Luci and her children to apply for other coverage to be effective October 1. After maintaining coverage their entire lives they were uninsured.

Tricia and I collaborated and our firm filed complaints with the Attorney General's Office and through the Insurance Department. Our work led ConnectiCare to extend coverage to the family for one additional month. However, our efforts to extend coverage while Luci worked in the business to bring it to closure were unsuccessful.

We had to act quickly so that new coverage would be in force for November 1. Fortunately, everyone in the family was healthy. Tricia and I discussed options and Anthem Blue Cross and Blue Shield looked attractive but it made much more sense for all three Watsons to apply for coverage as individuals rather than as a family. Connecticut, like most states has "age-rated" premiums so premiums are lower for young, healthy people. Also, there was no "parent and children" rate at the time and if Luci had applied for family coverage, the family premium would have been based on her age and far more expensive than the three individual premiums combined.

The applications for Taylor (daughter) and Jamie (son) Watson flew through the approval process. Unfortunately, feedback Tricia Daigle, the broker, received from the Anthem underwriting department was that Luci's application was being held up for further review since she had attended grief counseling sessions after David had died. We collaborated with the broker to intensify our efforts to inform the insurer that Luci's grief therapy was related to her husband's recent tragic and sudden death and was not an indication

Mailing Address:
175 Scott Swamp Road
Farmington, CT 06032-3124
(860) 674-5700

ConnectiCare, Inc. & Affiliates

September 30, 2005

Re: David Watson Consulting

Group #:D07273

Dear Patricia:

I am responding to your question regarding continuation of coverage for the spouse and child of the decedent employee in a one-life group. Since the decedent was the only employee covered under the group, then the group ceased to exist when he died. COBRA is a continuation of benefits under a group policy that continues in force, so COBRA is not available where there is no group policy to continue benefits from. Also, ConnectiCare's business rules do not permit COBRA–only group. There maybe someone winding down the business, but since it has no employees, it cannot provide group coverage. Termination will be September 30th, and October premium will be returned. Since our group policies have no conversion feature, there is no conversion to an individual plan available. I have mailed a ConnectiCare Solo enrollment kit to Luci Watson in case she would like to consider applying. However, please advise client that it will be medically underwritten and coverage is not guaranteed issue.
Please let me know if I can be of any assistance.

Sincerely,

One Farmglen Boulevard, Farmington, CT 06032
www.connecticare.com

ConnectiCare response to broker stating
no **COBRA** extension provided to surviving
family members after death of husband.

of underlying chronic mental illness. Needless to say, we also threatened them with appeals, potential litigation and ugly public relations activities should they consider denying coverage for this otherwise healthy widow. Luci's coverage was approved.

Sole proprietor coverage can be a very good option for many people. In a situation where the sole proprietor suddenly dies, however, the lack of any COBRA protection can lead to ruthlessly abrupt termination of coverage for any dependents. You can't rely on an insurer to make an exception. Anyone with sole proprietor coverage for a spouse or family needs to understand this risk.

Moving to a Different State

Joanne Yamamoto was a self-employed consultant in Los Angeles who had purchased her own individual insurance policy years ago. She assumed the insurance would provide good protection. After all, it wasn't cheap. In fact, in 2009 the policy premium was $514.92 per month. At age 60, Joanne was diagnosed with aggressive cancer and learned that the policy for which she'd paid so dearly actually had many payment limitations. During one 12 day admission to UCLA Medical Center, room and board charges were about $4,000.00/day but her insurance had a payment limit of $400.00/day. Even though she had insurance, hospital staff once counseled her on how to discharge herself, against medical advice, because she couldn't immediately pay the large balance due on her hospital bill. Over time, Joanne ended up with six figure bills from hospitals and doctors.

Joanne couldn't obtain other coverage. There was no sole proprietor coverage in California and she couldn't qualify for better individual coverage now that she had such serious illness. She was ineligible to apply to the California Major Risk Medical Insurance program, California's Program for people who cannot get private individual insurance due to pre-existing conditions. According to the Program's rules, you aren't eligible for that coverage if you already have coverage, even if your existing coverage isn't very good.

Over time, due to her illness, Joanne was unable to continue the level of consulting activity she had in the past so her financial situation had become grim. Because she couldn't afford to remain in Los Angeles, she moved across the country to live with a friend in North Carolina. In 2009, North Carolina established a High Risk Pool Program for residents. Once Joanne had established residency in North Carolina, she was eligible for coverage through this program which allowed her to give up the rather limited coverage she had. She received outstanding care at Duke Medical Center and had extremely comprehensive coverage protection.

Do I have your attention? I hope so.

MORE ON CLUELESS ABOUT COVERAGE...

In spite of all the turmoil and change in the healthcare field, the majority of Americans do enjoy good healthcare coverage. Most Americans are covered through a group such as an employer or union and 47 million more are on Medicare. Coverage through a larger employer is typically the most sought after. That coverage can be heavily subsidized for all family members and with enough tenure, many large companies offer medical coverage after retirement.

In many ways, good coverage through an employer or union is both a blessing and a curse—a blessing because the coverage is often heavily subsidized by the group; a curse because as long as someone else, like an employer, is managing these matters for us, we tend to remain clueless about coverage and its cost. We are, in a very real sense, "coverage illiterate." Also, most of us don't control whether or not we remain employed. Employers of all sizes continue to look to reduce staff and outsource work, putting us at risk of losing our healthcare coverage. Most laid off employees have a temporary safety net through COBRA (paying for group coverage yourself) but COBRA can be shockingly expensive.

Many of the transitions that affect medical coverage are extremely painful—job loss, divorce and death of a spouse. We are preoccupied with the very event causing the transition so find it difficult to devote the energy necessary to planning a coverage transition. Ironically, other coverage transitions are exceedingly joyous—moving to a part of the country you always wanted to live in or retirement after a long, productive career. Sometimes even the most joyous transitions can be associated with insurance traps because state insurance environments vary so widely. Again, regardless of your circumstance, thoughtful, strategic planning and thorough research for every affected family member are highly recommended when facing a coverage transition.

BIRTH—THE FIRST COVERAGE TRANSITION

If you understand insurance you realize that birth is the first coverage transition. Newborns are eligible for temporary coverage when they are born as long as a parent has coverage but newborn children must be enrolled in a Plan for ongoing coverage. Hence, there are potential traps associated with our entry into the world and onto coverage. An enrollment form must be filled out properly and provided timely to either a benefits person, or broker or insurer—someone who adds the child to the policy. When this doesn't happen, claims can be denied. Often neither parent has thought about this very practical issue. At the other end of the age spectrum, Medicare enrollment has its own set of traps.

ELIGIBILITY AND ENROLLMENT

Two critical issues to understand in dealing with any type of insurance are eligibility and enrollment. When people run afoul of either or both of these issues, coverage may not be in effect. In the above example, a newborn infant of a parent with coverage is eligible for coverage. The trap comes when a parent does not properly enroll the child. Divorce is a particularly problematic transition. A divorced spouse is never eligible for coverage as a dependent but it is the responsibility of the subscriber or insured, often the ex-husband, to inform the employer of the divorce. As you can imagine, there can be a lack of good will left between two individuals at the end of a divorce process and proper notification can be problematic.

Medicare enrollment issues have also become increasingly complex. As a result, one may be eligible for Medicare but not have followed enrollment rules properly.

You must be eligible and enrolled to be entitled to health insurance benefits.

Whatever the circumstance in facing a coverage transition, the stakes are high. In a different era, coverage transitions weren't so perilous because both premiums and medical services cost relatively less. Years ago, even if you lost your group coverage, insurers generally offered you the option of converting to an individual policy and you could afford it! Even if you didn't have good coverage and had larger out-of-pocket costs, you could likely afford to pay for medical services. Imagine that. The world has changed. In today's environment, the cost of healthcare and healthcare coverage is a burden that causes much of the dysfunction described in this book.

In later chapters you will read about one client's $800,000.00 hospital bill ultimately reduced to (a mere) $500,000.00 after Medicare was exhausted, but still a staggering blow to the family. You have already read about one client who failed to obtain insurance after his COBRA ran out, incurring a $519,282.00 hospital bill in two months. The bill was ultimately reduced to $139,463.00, still a substantial sum for most of us. Back in 2001 we dealt with our first $1+ million hospital bill. This was a one-year-old baby taken to an in-network hospital emergency room due to a brain tumor and referred immediately by the pediatric neurologist to a university hospital deemed out-of-network.

I hope these figures grab your attention.

But let's talk about what should have been a minor matter—my husband's recent routine lab work done as part of his annual physical exam. The lab work was done at the local hospital which did not have his insurance information. Hospital charges for the lab work were $2,198.50 as you can see from the CIGNA explanation of benefit form on the opposite page. The Hospital thought my husband was uninsured so offered an uninsured patient discount bringing charges down to $1,319.10. The Hospital is actually in-network with my husband's insurer, so after I provided insurance information, payment in full was reduced to $90.78. My husband owed nothing. Have you followed me? The Hospital was seeking $1,319.10 from the uninsured or out-of-network patient in this scenario and claiming to extend a generous discount from their initial charges of $2,198.50. In actuality, the negotiated rate for payment in full was $90.78 from CIGNA.

Does it make any sense that hospital charges were 24 times the negotiated rate accepted as payment in full? Does it make any sense that the Hospital offered a "discount" off charges that were 14 times what CIGNA paid? No, it doesn't but that is the United States healthcare system. The likely hospital response to a question about the high charges would be that the Hospital is forced to accept low payment rates from Medicare and Medicaid and

Connecticut General Life Insurance Company
SCRANTON CLAIM OFFICE
P.O. BOX 182223
CHATTANOOGA TN 37422-7223

CIGNA

Connecticut General Life Insurance Company AS AGENT FOR CONSOLIDATED EDISON COMPANY OF NEW

Customer service
Call the number on the back of your ID card or
(800) 244-6224 (1.800.CIGNA24)
www.myCIGNA.com

If you have any questions about this document,
please call Customer Service at the number
above. Please have your reference number ready.

JOHN L CARLEY

DARIEN CT

Service date
November 1, 2010

THIS IS NOT A BILL.
Your health care professional may bill you directly
for any amount that you owe.

Reference # / ID
468 1034102889 / U38585253

Account name / Account #
CONSOLIDATED EDISON COMPANY OF NEW /
3331910

Explanation of benefits

for a claim received for JOHN L CARLEY, Reference # 468 1034102889

Summary of a claim for services on November 1, 2010

for services provided by STAMFORD HSP

Amount Billed	$2,198.50	This was the amount that was billed for your visit on 11/01/2010.
Discount	$2,107.72	**You saved $2,107.72.** CIGNA negotiates discounts with health care professionals and facilities to help you save money.
What CIGNA plan paid	$90.78	CIGNA paid $90.78 to STAMFORD HSP.
What I owe	$0.00	This is the amount you owe after your discount, what your CIGNA plan paid, and what your accounts paid. People usually owe because they may have a deductible, have to pay a percentage of the covered amount, or for care not covered by their plan. Any amount you paid since care was received may reduce the amount you owe
You saved	**100%**	You saved $2,198.50 (or 100%) off the total amount billed. This is a total of your discount and what your CIGNA plan paid. To maximize your savings, visit www.myCIGNA.com or call customer service to estimate treatment costs, or to compare cost and quality of in-network health care professionals and facilities.

H701A 7/09

PLEASE SEE CLAIM DETAILS ON PAGE 3.

Page 1 of 3

CIGNA explanation of benefit statement
showing $2198.50 In clinical laboratory
charges paid in full for $90.78.

STAMFORD HOSPITAL | The Regional Center for Health

Affiliate Columbia University College of Physicians & Surgeons
Member New York-Presbyterian Healthcare System
A Planetree Hospital

PO Box 5027
Stamford, CT 06904-5027
800-440-5238

November 19, 2010

John Leonard Carley

Darien CT

Patient:	John Leonard Carley
Patient #:	V00016658718
Account #:	3878014
Date of Service:	11/01/10
Insurance Listed:	

Please pay the balance due: $1319.10

Dear John Leonard Carley:

If you have insurance coverage that will pay your bill please call our office. You may need to contact your insurance company to authorize treatment. (Please check the instructions on your insurance card.)

Please fulfill your obligation by paying your balance due today. If payment has already been made, please accept our sincere thank you.

If you require information regarding your bill, please do not hesitate to call our office Monday through Thursday, 8:00 AM – 8:00 PM and Friday 8:00 AM – 5:00 PM. We are ready and willing to assist you. If paying by credit card, please note we currently accept VISA, MasterCard, American Express and Discover Card.

Please submit your payment to: Stamford Hospital
PO Box 5027
Stamford CT 06904-5027

The balance shown may reflect multiple account balances. Please contact our billing office for details regarding this bill.

We are attempting to collect a debt.

Billing Questions:	**(800) 440-5238**
Hours:	
8:00 A.M. – 8:00 P.M.	**Monday through Thursday**
8:00 A.M. – 5:00 P.M.	**Friday**

* * Please See Reverse Side For Important Information * *

44ONFIFI0130
REV. 08-04-09

Detach Lower Portion and Return with Payment

IF PAYING BY CREDIT CARD, COMPLETE ALL, SIGN AND RETURN	
☐ ☐ ☐ ☐ CHECK CARD USING FOR PAYMENT	
CARD NUMBER PLUS 3 DIGIT SECURITY CODE (on back of card)	EXP. DATE /
CARDHOLDER NAME	AMOUNT $
CARDHOLDER SIGNATURE	

PO Box 9317
Stamford CT 06904-9317
RETURN SERVICE REQUESTED

November 19, 2010

V00016658718-30   435669856

John Leonard Carley

Darien CT

STAMFORD HOSPITAL
PO Box 5027
Stamford CT 06904-5027

Amount Enclosed: $_____

Home: (_____)_____Work: (_____)_____

Account Number:	3878014
Patient Number:	V00016658718
Balance Due:	$1319.10

**Stamford Hospital Letter reducing $2198.50
in charges to $1319.10. (Payment in full from
CIGNA was $90.78.)**

provide a great deal of charity care for which they receive no payment. This is true. Hospital executives are well aware of our broken payment system.

Fortunately, my husband works for a large company that has the economic clout to negotiate favorable payment rates. But the question for all of us with good coverage is this: what are our options should we lose that good coverage? Many people suddenly become vulnerable by not realizing that during a coverage transition they can be exposed to substantial risks that they don't completely understand.

SHOPPING FOR COVERAGE ON YOUR OWN— BEWARE OF TRAPS

The most difficult situations often arise when someone shops for coverage on their own for the first time. A wide variety of events put individuals in that position. Since the federal health reform legislation, or ACA, turning 26 is one of them. Prior to ACA, turning 19 or discontinuing full-time student status triggered the end of coverage and a transition from a family's Plan.

In addition to turning 26, there are many other changes that can force a coverage transition. They include divorce, moving, job loss, death of a spouse, retirement, a spouse's retirement, your company being acquired, or exhausting COBRA benefits (a temporary extension of group benefits at the individual's expense).

People shopping for individual coverage for the first time can be overwhelmed and discouraged. Many insurance brokers don't want individuals or small groups as clients so individuals shop on-line where a variety of "pseudo" insurance products in addition to legitimate insurance products are available for purchase. Some insurance products just don't provide the protection one expects. Recall Joanne Yamamoto's individual policy, Moving Case Example, which had payment limitations on every significant claim. "Discount" programs parading as coverage are another trap. And then, of course, even if one homes in on the legitimate products highly regulated by State Insurance Departments, the options may seem unaffordable.

PRE-EXISTING CONDITIONS

Unfortunately, many Americans shopping for individual coverage for the first time learn that pre-existing conditions can be a reason for denial of health insurance in most states (at least until 2014 assuming the federal Affordable Care Act prevails). What is most shocking to people who've had good group coverage is that seemingly minor issues can lead to denial when applying for new insurance.

In the individual, private marketplace insurers have broad discretion to deny coverage (except in New York, New Jersey, Maine, Massachusetts and Vermont). Some insurers will add a surcharge to a premium for what they view as modest additional risk such as for someone who is overweight. Occasionally we see individual insurance issued with a specific exclusion but that is rare. Much more common is an outright denial. Most insurers in the private, individual marketplace are only looking to provide coverage to healthy individuals.

On page 54, you'll read about Rob and Marie. Marie's denial of coverage from Golden Rule stated: "We are unable to rider cholesterol problems." Although her health was good, she was denied coverage because she was taking Lipitor, a cholesterol drug.

Another client's application to Anthem Blue Cross and Blue Shield for individual coverage was denied based on "weight elevated relative to height." He was a very muscular gentleman who lifted weights. He appealed to Anthem and was ultimately approved. The insurer must give you a reason for the denial and you do have the right to appeal to the insurance company but the insurer has broad discretion to deny your application.

Another client was denied coverage for what his doctor stated in a letter was "slowly progressing arthritis of the hip well maintained by taking glucosamine and two Aleve at bedtime." This was an extremely active man working in a demanding position. His "slowly progressing arthritis" was not limiting his activities in any significant way. He appealed Anthem's denial and Anthem upheld the denial of coverage. As a result of the continued denial, this client had to remain on the state's High Risk Pool Plan. This man, who takes no prescription medications but does take glucosamine and Aleve, pays $1,874.00 per month for his health insurance, over $22,000.00 per year.

> *In all but five states, individual health insurance is medically underwritten, meaning the insurer may deny an application based on one's health.*

Yet another client's application for coverage to Anthem Blue Cross and Blue Shield was denied due to "knee sprain with symptoms and/or treatment within the last 30 days." This gentleman had a sprained knee, was referred to a physical therapist and had one visit. The appeal of his denial to Anthem was also denied. He obtained coverage through the state's High Risk Pool Plan. Various High Risk Pool Plan rates from California, Connecticut, Illinois, and Texas are included in the Appendix to this book. Unlike New York, rates in these states are age-rated. If you're older, you pay more—motivation enough to consider other types of insurance for which you might be eligible.

Certain medications also result in denials. If you're taking a drug for depression or anxiety, or are in any type of counseling, you will likely be denied insurance coverage in the private, individual marketplace. This is a terrible problem, in particular, for women getting divorced.

Regardless of someone's health, many insurance companies refuse to write insurance for entire professions including professional athletes, security guards, cab drivers, and window washers. In today's environment, the reality is that private insurance companies look to minimize their risk.

But even if you're a policyholder healthy enough to qualify for private, individual coverage, there are other perils to consider. Premiums can increase to levels that aren't affordable, you often can't take the coverage with you if you move out of state, and insurers go out of business or discontinue offering coverage in a given area, the dilemma Mr. and Mrs. Peters, page 18, faced.

Those transitions that don't necessarily involve "shopping" for coverage on your own but "choosing" among Plans an employer or union offers can also be extremely challenging. A practical problem is that we never know what the future might bring. Try to select a Plan that won't lead to remorse later. I can't count the times someone has spoken to me about their regret at choosing the Plan they did. The limited network Plan and/or the limited benefit Plan is fine when you are in good health but when someone in the family is diagnosed with cancer and the facility or doctors they want to go to are not in the network, or they can't get referrals to them, they are locked in to their current Plan until open enrollment.

MEDICARE

Another major transition in coverage is tied to enrolling in Medicare. For decades this was relatively uneventful. No more. Since 2006, Medicare has become much more complicated. Medicare doesn't have the same pre-existing condition issues that plague the non-Medicare world. However, Medicare enrollment rules are complex, unforgiving and punitive. Sometimes they ensnare those who've worked the longest, paid into the system for decades, and postponed Social Security and Medicare benefits.

Americans who enroll in Medicare during the General Enrollment Period (undesirable option of last resort) can face lifetime Medicare Part B premium penalties. Medicare also imposes a gap in coverage for those who enroll during the General Enrollment Period. Penalties and gaps in coverage are intended for those who are irresponsible—who don't pay in to the system and then want coverage when they're sick. But as enrollment issues have become more complex, our system has often trapped those who were ignorant of the complex rules, not because they were irresponsible or cavalier.

This book will help you assess your coverage and your options with a goal of maintaining comprehensive coverage through a private product or Medicare, to which most Americans are entitled at age 65. If you think you're eligible for Medicaid, a program for the indigent, or some other product associated with low income, you should contact your state Medical Assistance office. You can also call 1-800-MEDICARE (1-800-633-4227) and say "Medicaid" to obtain phone numbers for your state office.

ACA—The Patient Protection and Affordable Care Act of 2010 (Obamacare)

Some have asked, "How can you write a book about healthcare coverage when everything might change with ACA?" Not everything will change. No single piece of legislation will rationally transform our healthcare system over night.

Some provisions of ACA have already been implemented and are discussed in this book. Should ACA be fully implemented, the information presented here will be even more critical because for many Americans, healthcare coverage will become even more expensive.

ACA will benefit those who qualify for expanded Medicaid eligibility, other lower-income Americans who will qualify for subsidies for coverage, and the very wealthy who don't work or have access to group coverage through a spouse or parent and for whom the cost of premiums is not an issue.

Most of the options for healthcare coverage described in this book will remain whether reform is ultimately implemented or not. If state insurance exchanges for the purchase of individual and small group coverage operate as envisioned by ACA in 2014, then individuals will not be denied coverage due to pre-existing conditions.

The provisions of ACA will add to and continue to increase the cost of coverage because of the following:

+ Guaranteed individual coverage to children under 19 (in place)
+ Preventive care benefits at no out-of-pocket charge to the insured (in place)
+ Numerous caps on services, listed on page 41, including prescriptions drug and lifetime maximums removed (in place)

- Adult children up to age 26 can remain on a parent's Plan (in place)
- Insurance companies will not be able to write less expensive policies for healthy people (2014)

No one would argue against the desirability of protecting more Americans from the financial ruin of unanticipated medical bills but additional benefits result in additional cost. Without major reengineering of the way we provide, cover and pay for medical services, many people still will not be able to afford coverage.

OTHER REFORM EFFORTS

Massachusetts, the model for federal reform, has achieved success in being the state with the lowest percentage of uninsured. Reform in Massachusetts had broad political support but the state is struggling with the costs and premium increases associated with the program. The Pre-Existing Condition Insurance Plans created under ACA were launched in the third quarter of 2010. The Chief Actuary for Medicare and Medicaid estimated 375,000 people might enroll the first year. The Congressional Budget Office estimated 200,000 per year might enroll (*New York Times* editorial, February 16, 2011). As of August 31, 2011, 33,958 people were enrolled according to health.gov, a website managed by the U.S. Department of Health and Human Services. Do people not want healthcare coverage? I don't think so. For the most part, they're either uninformed, misinformed or don't believe they can afford it.

Much has been touted about ACA reducing the ranks of uninsured college grads. This is true, but prior to this reform provision taking place, almost everyone aging off a parent's Plan had a right to COBRA coverage for 36 months. Many couldn't afford COBRA so chose not to purchase it. The law has simply shifted most of the cost of covering young adults from individuals and families to employers. When more expense is shifted to employers, they often react by limiting benefits in some other manner or passing the costs shifted to them back to employees anyway. I would also like to point out that these newly insured young adults will still turn 26 one day, and will no longer be eligible for coverage under their parent's Plan.

Massachusetts universal healthcare is fairly new and Vermont's is newer still, but New York, New Jersey and Maine have a longer history with guaranteeing coverage for all residents without respect to health or pre-existing conditions. Let's look at New York. New York's program, passed in 1993, is a spectacular failure. New York rates for individual insurance are published monthly on the New York State Insurance Department website. December

2011 rates are on page 38. To view these rates go to http://www.dfs.ny.gov/insurance/hmorates/pdf/New_York.pdf.

Insurers in New York offer two Standard Individual Health Plans—an HMO with a limited network and a Point of Service Plan which includes out-of-network benefits. Rates for December 2011 ranged from a low of $866.57 per person per month with a HIP HMO, to a high of $1,932.00 per person per month with the Aetna Point of Service Plan. Aetna's family coverage with the out-of-network benefits is $5,975.00 per month as of December 2011. A family purchasing this coverage would pay Aetna $71,700.00 for one year of coverage. And how many families can afford that? New York provides guaranteed issue coverage without respect to pre-existing conditions but it hasn't worked because it is unaffordable.

ACA will eliminate pre-existing condition issues and add benefits but it will limit what insurers can charge. Medicare and Medicaid have a similar history. In order to pay for those programs, payments to those who provide care have been reduced. Reducing provider payments across the board isn't a viable long term solution. Indeed, it tends to increase the number of doctors who refuse to participate in Medicare and Medicaid.

INDIVIDUAL MANDATE

The controversial centerpiece of healthcare reform is the individual mandate—you buy comprehensive insurance or pay a penalty. This is the issue soon to be before the United States Supreme Court. The Supreme Court will also address whether the mandate is actually a tax which may mean that the mandate cannot be challenged until after it becomes effective in 2014.

The ACA penalties for not maintaining insurance are very modest relative to the cost of health insurance. Penalty amounts are phased in either as a flat fee, $95.00 in 2014, $325.00, in 2015 and $695.00 in 2016 or as a percentage of taxable household income, 1% in 2014, 2% in 2015 and 2.5% in 2016, whichever is greater. These are annual penalties which are slated to be increased by a-cost-of-living adjustment after 2016.

Many supporters of reform believe that by getting coverage for more healthy people, overall healthcare costs will decrease. This is not really accurate. With health insurance, additional benefits result in additional cost precisely because many services are discretionary. If forced to pay for coverage, you will use these services. This is the history of insurance and Medicare in our country.

I had a fascinating conversation with a life insurance professional who told me that bringing healthy people into a life insurance pool always results

Premium Rates for Standard Individual Health Plans
December 2011

Rates may vary depending upon the month in which you enroll.
To verify the rates listed below, please call applicable HMO directly.

New York County
(Manhattan)

HMO   **What You Pay Per Month**

Aetna Health, Inc.
800/435-8742

	HMO	POS
Individual	$1,261.00	$1,932.00
Husband/Wife	$2,522.00	$3,866.00
Parent & Child(ren)	$2,320.00	$3,558.00
Family	$3,898.00	$5,975.00

HMO   **What You Pay Per Month**

Empire HealthChoice HMO, Inc.
d/b/a Empire BlueCross BlueShield HMO
800/662-5193

	HMO	POS
Individual	$1,289.61	$1,611.27
Husband/Wife	$2,579.22	$3,222.54
Parent & Child(ren)	$2,398.67	$2,996.97
Family	$3,997.79	$4,994.94

HMO   **What You Pay Per Month**

Health Insurance Plan
of Greater New York, Inc.
800/447-8255

HMO			POS
Adult	$866.57	Individual	$1,486.46
Per Child *	$403.09	Husband/Wife	$2,972.91
* Maximum of $1,612.36 for 4 or more children.		Parent & children	$2,601.20
		Family	$4,283.84

HMO   **What You Pay Per Month**

Oxford Health Plans (NY), Inc.
800/216-0778

	HMO	POS
Individual	$1,259.77	$1,855.97
Husband/Wife	$2,519.54	$3,711.94
Parent & Child	$2,534.66	$3,734.21
Family	$3,873.79	$5,707.11

HMO   **What You Pay Per Month**

Atlantis Health Plan, Inc.
866/747-8422

	HMO	POS
Individual	$1,025.80	$1,710.72
Husband/Wife	$2,051.60	$3,421.44
Parent & Child(ren)	$2,010.57	$3,353.02
Family	$3,077.40	$5,132.17

HMO   **What You Pay Per Month**

GHI HMO Select, Inc.
d/b/a GHI HMO
914/340-2300
877/244-4466

	HMO	POS
Individual	$2,765.60	$3,318.77
Family	$7,052.27	$8,462.86

HMO   **What You Pay Per Month**

Managed Health, Inc.
d/b/a HealthFirst New York
888/260-1010

	HMO	POS
Individual	$1,116.74	$1,532.28
Husband/Wife	$2,232.28	$3,063.07
Parent & Child(ren)	$1,975.49	$2,710.59
Family	$3,316.56	$4,550.94

New York City Individual Insurances Rates,
December 2011

in reduced premiums. Well, that is because people have to die to access life insurance benefits and we don't choose to die. We buy auto insurance but don't choose to get in to auto accidents. We buy homeowners insurance but don't choose to have our house burn down. Healthcare is fundamentally different. We do choose to use health services, as we should.

This is not to argue that everyone shouldn't have coverage. My point is solely that the history of health insurance is that benefits drive utilization and when more people are covered, costs ultimately increase. Achieving progress toward the important objective of universal coverage with a core benefit package seems far more sensible to me and potentially far more successful than the ACA approach. What is the point of mandating comprehensive benefits when many will opt to pay a penalty rather than purchase that coverage due to the cost?

INSURANCE EXCHANGE

One aspect of the recent federal legislation taken from Massachusetts is the creation of a "health insurance exchange" in each state. A "health insurance exchange" is an agency which oversees which state-regulated Plans will be offered to individuals and small groups.

The idea of an exchange is very positive because it is intended to make shopping for products, including online shopping, in a complex healthcare world more transparent. However, based on our experience in Massachusetts it's not quite that simple. The information provided on the Massachusetts Health Connector isn't necessarily in sync with information on local insurance Plan websites. The Connector website categorizes options into Bronze, Silver and Gold. The terminology on the Connector website doesn't match what insurers call their various Plans listed on Plan websites. I urge you to go to the Massachusetts Connector, www.mahealthconnector.org, and use the Find a Plan tool. I used a Boston area zip code with my date of birth. I can choose from 12 bronze Plans, eight silver Plans and four gold Plans. This is transparency? This is easy? Most Americans, especially those who've enjoyed coverage through an employer most of their lives, are not prepared to evaluate and choose among more than 20 different health Plans.

Until recently, all our clients in Massachusetts had either individual or group insurance in place. I'd like to share our experience with a recent client, another small business owner in Massachusetts. He had moved to Massachusetts and kept his limited insurance policy from another state. He was being fined by Massachusetts because his coverage wasn't considered comprehensive enough. He had looked at buying more comprehensive coverage but didn't believe he could afford it.

A surprising development in our recent dealings with this Massachusetts small business owner was that according to the Massachusetts Health Connector website (the exchange) and staff, he had only one choice of health Plan, a local Plan. The good news was that the Plan had been in business since 1986 so had a track record. NONE of the family's primary care physicians participated in that Plan, however. According to the Connector staff he had to buy this insurance or be fined. When we contacted a reputable broker in the area, he stated that we'd been given misinformation by the Connector representative. The client, according to the broker, could actually have access to all the prominent, well-known Plans in the Boston area. In fact, our client obtained coverage through the broker with Harvard Pilgrim Health Plan which the Connector staff had stated was not an option. Before we contacted the broker, the client was actually considering obtaining individual coverage for his family and his one employee for which he would also be fined (because as an employer in Massachusetts he must offer employer coverage), rather than be limited to the one small group Plan offered in his zip code. This was not an easy process for this small business owner (or for us).

This Massachusetts client faced the same dilemma many hard-working (but not eligible for a subsidy) Americans face. He can be assured in Massachusetts that any policy he purchases through the Connector will be good comprehensive protection. Massachusetts residents won't be surprised like Joanne Yamamoto, page 25, was. That reassurance, however, isn't very productive if families choose to pay a penalty they can afford rather than coverage they cannot afford.

What is not yet clear about ACA is how pre-existing condition issues will be dealt with if someone chooses to pay the penalty rather than obtain coverage. An insurer usually can impose a pre-existing condition exclusion, or waiting period, when an individual has not maintained continuous coverage. The threat of an exclusion is intended to encourage people to be responsible and maintain coverage. Yet there is a part of the ACA legislation that creates a temporary pre-existing condition High Risk Pool. However, an individual is not eligible unless he or she has been uninsured for at least six months. This provision is terribly unfair to those who've struggled to pay existing State High Risk Pool premiums, for conversion options, or other expensive guaranteed issue coverage options typically at substantially higher rates. How sensible is this?

MORE UNLIMITED BENEFITS

Another ACA concern is that businesses and insurers are forced to assume so much additional financial risk. Businesses which offer healthcare coverage must now provide **unlimited lifetime maximums** for a number of services such as:

+ Ambulatory patient services
+ Emergency services
+ Hospitalization
+ Maternity and newborn care
+ Mental health and substance use disorder services
+ Prescription drugs
+ Rehabilitative services and devices
+ Laboratory services
+ Preventive and wellness services and chronic disease management
+ Pediatric services

Ironically, ACA requires non-Medicare Plans to offer unlimited hospitalization benefits, for example, when Medicare, our country's federal healthcare program, does not. Please read about this in our Medicare Traps and Gaps section. Several years ago we worked with a *Fortune* 100 Company painfully deliberating over whether to increase the lifetime maximum for its employees from $1 million to $1,250,000 which they finally did. Now, as a result of ACA, they must absorb many unlimited annual and lifetime maximums.

*The Patient Protection and Affordable Care Act of 2010 requires **unlimited** lifetime maximums on key benefits like prescription drugs. Now some Plans exclude drug coverage or include 50% co-insurance for drugs.*

We have dealt with the tragedy of those approaching a lifetime maximum and it's horrible. But forcing companies to take on much more financial risk will lead them to seek ways to reduce risk elsewhere. Hence we see higher and higher deductibles and co-insurance. For example, more Plans have instituted a 50% co-insurance for the prescription drug benefit. Historically, the co-pay for prescription drugs has been a fixed amount/three tier co-pay structure. Similarly, we are seeing self-insured employers administer COBRA in an unforgiving and harsh manner. A late payment can result in your COBRA coverage being terminated because the employer doesn't want to assume risk associated with a former employee or his or her dependents.

Medicare existed for 40 years before an outpatient drug benefit was added in 2006. People on Medicare before 2006 got drug coverage through a former employer or a Medicare Supplement they bought themselves or a private Medicare Advantage Plan. But just a few years after the government finally added a limited Medicare outpatient drug benefit, ACA requires employers and insurers to provide unlimited drug coverage. Yet we wonder why business isn't racing to create more jobs.

ACCOUNTABLE CARE ORGANIZATIONS

Of course, any legislation as massive as the ACA has positive elements in it as well. The legislation includes creation of Accountable Care Organizations (ACOs). Very simply, the objective of ACOs is to encourage more appropriate use of precious medical resources by paying providers who work together to deliver high quality, coordinated medical services. ACOs are intended to improve care to Medicare beneficiaries by bundling payments to providers who can demonstrate they provide effective services. We should all hope some of these projects will be successful and serve as a model for others.

The legislation also includes a rating system which will provide for higher payments to Medicare Advantage and Medicare Part D Plans that have a track record of providing quality care and service. It also provides for a Special Enrollment Period for them. There are concerns about "gaming the system" but rating Medicare Plans is a move in the right direction if it results in consumers being able to identify high quality options.

JPMorgan Chase & Co.

August 19, 2011

We are in receipt of your letter dated July 14, 2011 inquiring into the reinstatement of your COBRA coverage. Any decision to accommodate your request is based on our review of your records, as well as, plan requirements and provisions.

We have determined the coverage was terminated due to non-payment. A review of your record shows:

- COBRA elections were made May 3, 2011 with the first payment due June 17, 2011.
- May 10, 2011 Billing Notice generated for May and June premiums in the amount of $1,024.52. May's premiums would be due by the above deadline, June 17, 2011.

Your letter indicates you missed making your payment as you did not have your mail forwarded to your new address. It is the COBRA participant's responsibility to pay the monthly premiums, in a timely fashion, whether an invoice is received or not. As a courtesy, JPMorgan Chase provides invoices to our COBRA participants; however, we are not obligated to do so. According to COBRA guidelines, set forth by the U.S. Department of Labor and IRS, and your COBRA notification package; it is the responsibility of the COBRA recipient to make sure that monthly premium payments are made in a timely manner. You may view these guidelines at www.dol.gov.

If a premium payment is not received by the required deadline, benefits are terminated retroactively to the last day of the month in which a full premium payment was received Because your COBRA payment was not received by the required deadline; we are unable to reinstate coverage.

While I realize this is not the response you had hoped for, I trust you realize the need to administer the program on a consistent basis for all participants.

Sincerely,

JPMorgan Chase, Corporate Benefits

JPMorgan Chase Corporate Benefits

Phoenix, AZ 85001

Letter to prospective COBRA recipient stating no exceptions made for missing first payment.

Your Coverage Plan

Amerian families have all kinds of plans—financial plans, college plans—why not Coverage Plans? We need to ask ourselves the question, *"What if I lose my healthcare coverage or what if something happens to disrupt it?"* and have some idea what the answer would be. You need a Coverage Plan. As you'll see, Coverage Plans can be involved and complicated because there are numerous options with different advantages and disadvantages. Other times, Coverage Plans are simple. My plan is simple. My husband works for a large electric utility in New York that provides good group benefits which, like most coverage from a large employer, is heavily subsidized by his employer. I am on the Plan as a spouse and intend to stay married and on the Plan. Should we get divorced, unlikely after 29 years of marriage but possible, divorce is a qualifying event (see terms in Appendix), I could elect COBRA and would have to consider my other options including getting coverage through Healthcare Navigation, my business.

> *A Coverage Plan makes you answer the question, "What if I lose my healthcare coverage?"*

Should my husband pass away before he retires, also unlikely because he's very healthy but always possible, I have to determine whether his company would provide survivor benefits to me. Survivor benefits are associated with retiree coverage. Should my husband die unexpectedly, the question would be whether I'd be entitled to survivor benefits because he would have been eligible for retiree medical, or whether I would only be eligible for COBRA. Getting clear answers to these questions can be harder than you might think. Worst case in this scenario is that I would get a lovely letter of condolence like so many others I've seen to new widows which ends by stating, "By the way, you will be terminated from the group health Plan at the end of the month but will have a right to elect COBRA."

When the day comes that I am eligible for Medicare at age 65, if my husband is still working for his large company, I may not need Medicare but will likely enroll in Medicare Part A. I will be entitled to premium-free Part A under current rules because I paid Social Security payroll taxes the required number of years. When either of us retires, we'll have other Medicare coverage issues to address, discussed in the Medicare portion of this book. Since my husband and I are close in age, our Coverage Planning challenges are simpler than they would be for couples where the older spouse might age onto Medicare, but the younger spouse might lose group coverage after COBRA is exhausted and be too young for Medicare.

Having a Coverage Plan doesn't mean having a formal, written document but rather thinking through the "what ifs" very, very strategically for every family member. All family members don't have to have the same coverage. Often it will be to your benefit not to. Remember the Watson family. They paid much less for the SAME coverage by applying as individuals rather than as a family. Do your homework. It is distressing to interact with people who would put more thought into the purchase of a household appliance than they would their family's healthcare coverage issues.

But healthcare coverage planning isn't easy. Far from it, the field is hurdling in a direction of becoming increasingly complex.

Q&A:
Key Laws and Terms

As painful as it may be, everyone should become familiar with basic health, health insurance terms and acronyms. There is an entire section of the book in the Appendix on federal laws and terms you should know. To entice you to read that section, I am including some background information and a case study that I hope will intrigue you and motivate you to become familiar with the terms and definitions that follow in the Appendix.

Healthcare and healthcare coverage has its own language. How many times have I heard "Who could know this stuff?" **You can** because we're going to make it just as straightforward as possible.

What should I know about State Insurance Departments?
Let's start with some key legislation and background. Most insurance products are regulated by State Insurance Departments but state environments vary much more widely than most people realize. In fact, states can seem like different galaxies. This is a terrible problem in the United States because so many people have no idea that moving from state to state can affect your healthcare coverage. Insurance products regulated by states are "fully-insured" meaning the premium is paid and the insurer assumes the risk for paying claims. If you have coverage regulated by your state, then the State Insurance Department may be a good source of information for you and in case of a dispute, you probably have a right to appeal, complain or file a grievance with the State Insurance Department.

What should I know about self-insured Plans?

Larger companies tend to be regulated under federal law because this allows them flexibility in designing their coverage. Companies with employees in several states often don't want to deal with varying state laws so they "self-insure" or pay insurance claims to a certain level and hire an insurer to process claims for them. These Plans are regulated under federal law known as the Employment Retirement Income Security Act (ERISA), defined in the Appendix.

How can you know if your coverage is regulated by your state or the federal government? You can't tell from your insurance card. If you have a benefits booklet or policy, look in the appeals section. Generally, if the appeals section indicates you can appeal a dispute up to the State Insurance Department, then you have coverage regulated by your state. If the appeals section of your booklet indicates that in a dispute you can file a complaint with the U.S. Labor Department, then your Plan is regulated by the federal government.

You should always know whether the state or federal government regulates your Plan because you do want to know how to proceed if a dispute should arise. Also, if you have coverage regulated by a state, you want to know that your Plan includes the benefits the state mandates.

A number of federal laws are also critically important in terms of how they affect coverage and coverage transitions. COBRA and HIPAA, explained in a simplified way below, are federal laws that provide protection for those going from one source of group coverage to a different source of group coverage or from exhausting COBRA coverage to whatever program your state has established for coverage of individuals with pre-existing conditions in that state.

What should I know about COBRA and HIPAA protections?

The combination of protections through COBRA, federal legislation enacted in 1986, and HIPAA, federal legislation passed in 1996, guarantees access to coverage for almost every American who has had coverage through a job or a dependent who has coverage tied to a job. So—if almost everyone who has coverage through a job has a right to continue that coverage through COBRA and then when COBRA is exhausted has the right to convert to other coverage through HIPAA, why are so many people uninsured? It's primarily the cost. They either can't afford it or feel they can't afford it. Nevertheless, it is critically important to understand the important coverage protections provided by these two federal laws.

COBRA and HIPAA protections aren't relevant if you already have private, individual coverage you pay for yourself. There also is no COBRA with individual coverage. As we learned with David Watson in the opening of the book, there is no COBRA coverage with a sole proprietor Plan either. Individual coverage is governed by state laws and is often tied to your state of residence. That is why moving to another state can be problematic with individual coverage.

THE DEFINITIONS WHICH FOLLOW ARE SIMPLIFIED.

What is COBRA?
COBRA is part of federal legislation, The Consolidated Omnibus Reconciliation Act of 1985, which provides for a temporary extension of group insurance benefits at the former employee's or dependent's cost. According to federal law, most employers with 20 or more employees must offer COBRA. Many states have a similar program for smaller employers, often referred to as "mini-COBRA." Check with your State Insurance Department to determine what a small employer must provide because the length of the COBRA period may be shorter under your State's law.

Why was COBRA passed and whom does it help?
COBRA provides a coverage safety net to enable a person losing group coverage to bridge that transition to other coverage options while being protected from any pre-existing condition exclusion problems.

So-called "Qualifying Events" entitle one to COBRA. As a worker, qualifying events are:
+ Loss of employment for other than gross misconduct
+ Reduction in work hours making you ineligible for the Plan

COBRA (temporary coverage) and HIPAA, (guaranteed conversion to coverage at end of COBRA) are intended to provide almost all Americans access to healthcare coverage.

A spouse also has a COBRA right based on the above, as well as additional rights in the event of:

+ Employee becoming entitled to Medicare
+ Divorce
+ Death of a spouse

Dependents used to age off a parent's Plan at 19 or when they were no longer a full time student. As discussed previously, adult children can now stay on a parent's Plan to age 26 as long as they are not eligible for group coverage through work. At age 26, those adult children also have a COBRA right. Some states have higher age limits for staying on a parent's Plan. New Jersey's is 31. Age isn't the only criterion. States tend to have less liberal guidelines than the federal law relating to marital status, financial support and residency. If this is important to you, check the specifics of your state's requirements.

If COBRA is such an important protection, what's the problem?
The most vexing problem with COBRA is cost. Premiums are often unaffordable for all but the affluent. Because most of us have relatively good health and relatively good group coverage subsidized by an employer for most of our lives, we remain ignorant about the true cost of coverage. When we're offered COBRA, a type of "COBRA sticker-shock" sets in and what was supposed to be an important safety net is often declined.

How expensive is COBRA?
COBRA rates vary dramatically because group coverage rates vary dramatically. Rates are generally a function of the richness of the health benefits and the age and health of the pool of people upon which the rates are based. COBRA rates for an individual typically fall in a range between a $400.00 and $1,000.00 per month for an individual.

How long does COBRA last?
For the worker, COBRA usually lasts for up to 18 months. For dependents losing coverage, including 26-year-olds aging off, a divorced spouse or family of a deceased spouse, COBRA can extend for up to 36 months. Those who become disabled while on COBRA can usually be on COBRA for 29 months to bring them to the date they'll likely be eligible for Medicare through disability.

What else do I need to know about COBRA?

Temporary: Even if it's affordable, COBRA is not always the wisest coverage option because it's temporary. Individual coverage in most states today (which is supposed to change in 2014 due to ACA) is medically underwritten. That means you fill out a questionnaire about your health and if you're not very healthy, or the insurer sees too much risk in your history, or because of the medications you take, you may be denied coverage. Some who will qualify for individual coverage are better off selecting individual coverage rather than risking developing a pre-existing condition while on COBRA which might make them ineligible for private individual coverage when COBRA is exhausted. After all, we still don't know what's going to happen in 2014 and whether health insurance will be made available to all regardless of health status.

Tied to group: In today's economy, many businesses have failed. One's fate is tied to the company through which COBRA was granted. If the company goes out of business as Mr. Peters' company did, there is no COBRA. If the company only offers an HMO Plan with a network tied to a specific geographic area and you want to move away, you may not meet the eligibility requirements of the Plan. Even if you can keep the Plan just for urgent and emergent care coverage, it may not be worth the price.

Timeframe for election: If you're leaving a job, employers handle the notice and the person with the COBRA option has 60 days to decide whether to take COBRA. In a situation like divorce, the person with the coverage who is getting divorced needs to notify the administrator or employer to start the process.

> *COBRA is temporary. Plan ahead*
> *for your next health insurance transition.*

Complying with notices and paying premiums: Don't ever be cavalier about responding timely to COBRA notices or paying premiums on time. Save all documentation. We are seeing more and more absolutely rigid administration of COBRA meaning if you don't follow the rules and pay premiums on time, your COBRA coverage will be terminated. There is no grace period. In today's environment, many employers, particularly self-insured employers (see Appendix for definition), know that having to keep a newly divorced person or newly widowed person on their Plan for three additional years with unlimited lifetime caps on hospitalization or drugs is an enormous potential risk and employers will limit that risk if you give them the opportunity. Make a late payment and they may cancel you.

Planning: Opting for COBRA can be of vital importance. However, in my experience opting for COBRA often results in postponement of planning for future coverage options. A very common but unfortunate call to our office is, "My COBRA is expiring next week and I need to know what to do." Often, it is too late to do much. In our view, you shouldn't elect COBRA without knowing it is your wisest choice and you shouldn't wait until the end of COBRA to plan your next source of coverage.

What is the Health Insurance Portability and Accountability Act (HIPAA)?
The Health Insurance Portability and Accountability Act (HIPAA) of 1996 is better known for its protections related to privacy of our medical information. However, HIPAA provides the following as long as you don't have a gap in group coverage of 63 days or longer:
+ Protection from a current group Plan imposing
  pre-existing condition exclusions
+ Guaranteed right to go from one group Plan to another group Plan
  (usually changing jobs) without the new Plan imposing pre-existing
  condition exclusions (not paying claims associated with illness
  or injury)
+ Guaranteed right to transition from the end of COBRA to whatever
  coverage your state has designated for "HIPAA-eligible" people

It is HIPAA that requires your insurance company to issue a "letter of creditable coverage" after your coverage terminates. Letters of creditable coverage indicate when coverage started and when it ended. One of the original goals of HIPAA was to ensure that people wouldn't stay in a job just to avoid changing coverage and the risk of a pre-existing condition being imposed.

Very simply, the term HIPAA-eligible means you've had 18 months of continuous group coverage without a break of 63 days or more. The combination of COBRA and HIPAA is intended to provide every American who had coverage tied in some way to employment to have guaranteed coverage essentially to age 65 and Medicare. It just hasn't worked out that way. This is largely because the cost of both COBRA and the HIPAA conversion option can be prohibitive and, for many, periods of unemployment have been lengthy.

What else do I need to know about portability and HIPAA?
State approaches to meeting HIPAA portability requirements vary for those exhausting COBRA and purchasing individual coverage. In some states individual insurance is guaranteed issue meaning you apply and are entitled to the insurance based on residency rather than health status. New York, New Jersey, Maine and Massachusetts (the model for the current federal reform legislation), and more recently, Vermont, maintain this approach to individual coverage.

Many states, 34 at last count, including California, Illinois, Texas, Indiana and Connecticut have so-called High Risk Pool Programs. Other states like Florida, Georgia, Michigan and Nevada, provide for a conversion to an individual policy when COBRA is exhausted. It is always extremely important to research what you are entitled to in your state because the ground rules can change.

> *Five states provide guaranteed issue individual coverage; 34 states have High Risk Pool Programs for individuals who can't get private, individual insurance; 11 states have a guaranteed conversion program when COBRA is exhausted.*

Again, these portability protections DO NOT apply to someone who has individual coverage. By definition, if you have individual coverage you pay for and do not have coverage through a group, then you can't be "HIPAA-eligible." This is a confusing but important. You might have individual coverage that is considered comprehensive so that it's deemed "creditable" but should you lose that coverage for whatever reason, you are not "HIPAA-eligible."

Remember, Mr. and Mrs. Peters lost their COBRA when Mr. Peters' former employer went out of business. When they lost their COBRA, Mr. and Mrs. Peters were HIPAA-eligible individuals. They then chose to buy individual coverage in their state. When that insurance company decided to leave the state and Mr. Peters had developed a pre-existing condition, he was not a HIPAA-eligible person even though he had "creditable coverage." In Mr. Peters' state of Connecticut, there is an option for non-HIPAA-eligible people to get coverage through the Health Reinsurance Association or high risk pool program if one acts timely, but this is not true in all states. Again, state insurance environments vary widely.

Portability—the ability to move your coverage when you move—is an enormous problem with this country's current approach to coverage. HIPAA was intended to address this problem but instead it largely benefits those moving from group to group coverage. If you exhaust COBRA and convert to your state's program for HIPAA-eligible individuals, you may face difficulty should you want to move to another state, depending on the state. Ironically, your coverage is often not "portable."

What is a waiting period?
An employer or group Plan has the right to specify a waiting period before benefits begin for new employees. During the waiting period, healthcare coverage benefits through the new employer are not in place. Not realizing how long the waiting period may be, or taking an extended break between jobs without taking COBRA, can lead to a break in coverage that can be problematic if you have a pre-existing condition or one develops. A pre-existing condition is generally defined as a condition for which medical advice, diagnosis, care, or treatment was recommended or received during the six-month period prior to an individual's enrollment date. Again, the ideal situation is to never have a gap in coverage.

We have been involved in many disputes regarding pre-existing conditions. Some have been absurd. One month after a healthy one year old physical, a baby was diagnosed with a brain tumor and the insurer tried to deny coverage. Clearly, the tumor had been growing but was entirely undetected by doctors prior to the brain tumor being diagnosed. The family had continuous coverage.

Another insurer tried to deny my son Paul's coverage due to a pre-existing condition even though he has had continuous group coverage his entire life. Go to page 96 to read about that situation.

Individual insurance and group insurance are different. You are well protected from pre-existing condition issues if you go from group coverage to group coverage without a gap. Not so with individual coverage in the private marketplace. In most states the insurer can reject your application for coverage if they feel there is too much risk due to your pre-existing condition(s).

You should also know that if you have a pre-existing condition or a health condition for which you haven't sought treatment and lie about it on an insurance application, the insurer usually has the right to rescind your coverage within the first two years if it is discovered you weren't truthful. We've known many people desperate enough to lie about their health status on an insurance application. We understand the desperation but lying on an insurance application is insurance fraud. It is terribly unfortunate that so many Americans who lose their group coverage are left with no good options for coverage.

Finally, please know that if you've had group coverage for 18 months, your insurer should not deny claims due to a pre-existing condition issue.

Summary: HIPAA is an important protection against the imposition of pre-existing condition exclusions for people losing group coverage or finishing COBRA. With ACA, pre-existing condition exclusions may go away in 2014 although there may be a waiting period for those who choose to remain uninsured. When you become eligible for Medicare, pre-existing conditions don't matter but depending on the state, pre-existing conditions can affect your Medicare supplemental Plan if you purchased it outside of the appropriate Enrollment Period. For more information, please read the Medicare section of the book.

COBRA, HIPAA and
State Environments

Rob was an executive who took COBRA for himself and his wife, Marie, when he retired in Nevada since he was not old enough for Medicare and the company offered no retiree medical coverage. He assumed that he and his wife would apply for individual coverage and get it when the COBRA expired. To his shock, both he and Marie were denied coverage when they applied which led to Rob's call to us. We were a little surprised at Marie's denial. She was taking Lipitor but was otherwise a totally healthy woman in her 50s. Rob recently had a basal cell carcinoma growth removed from his arm. He was denied individual coverage, too. Part of the problem is that when Rob applied for coverage on-line, he had used the wrong term and described a much more serious type of skin cancer than the basal cell growth he had recently had removed. This greatly complicated the situation because he didn't have the more aggressive cancer he described and any application for health insurance which is medically underwritten (only granted based on good health) includes the question, "Have you ever been denied insurance coverage?" and these questions must be answered truthfully.

Rob and Marie were residents of Nevada which offered conversion coverage at the end of COBRA to HIPAA-eligible individuals but the conversion coverage was expensive. Also of note, Rob and Marie were in the midst of deciding to make their second home in Texas their permanent residence. We felt they shouldn't consider Nevada conversion coverage if they were planning to change their permanent residence.

Rob and Marie ultimately decided to make Texas their primary residence. Texas has a High Risk Pool Program but Rob and Marie thought they'd be better off obtaining individual insurance coverage in Texas if they could qualify. The High Risk Pool Program existed to extend coverage to people who couldn't get insurance in the individual market and so would be more expensive.

Marie had no problems obtaining individual coverage in Texas in spite of taking Lipitor and admitting that she'd been denied coverage in Nevada. Rob's situation was more complicated. Customer service representatives at the insurance company were discouraging because his basal cell removal was recent. They said any basal cell removal within two months of an application would lead the application to be automatically denied, but Rob decided to apply anyway. Rob had to provide the medical records that proved he didn't have a more serious type of skin cancer. Due to timing, Rob filed an application for individual insurance but also applied to the High Risk Pool Program as a "back-up" option in case he was denied individual insurance. In spite of the insurer customer services representatives advising he would likely be denied, Rob's application for individual insurance was accepted. He was also accepted by the Texas High Risk Pool Program since he had a previous insurance denial. The Program didn't charge him for that first month's coverage and returned his check. What a process.

In sum, Rob and his wife were both denied private, individual insurance in Nevada but approved in Texas. State environments vary and underwriting criteria across insurance companies differ and can change.

Transition Traps and Gaps When Losing Coverage

Most forced coverage transitions occur due to loss of group coverage. Group coverage means just that—you are part of a covered group, usually through an employer or a union. If it is a larger group, most of the cost of the coverage is typically paid for by the group. As discussed previously, when you lose that coverage you are often ignorant of how much group coverage can cost. You may also have never had to purchase coverage on your own, so you're not ideally suited to be an informed buyer.

Going from one source of group coverage to another source of group coverage, typically changing jobs or going on a spouse's Plan, has its perils as discussed later but the perils of losing your good group coverage for the first time tend to be more traumatic.

KNOW YOUR OPTIONS AND ADVANTAGES AND DISADVANTAGES OF EACH

When you're losing group coverage, you may have a number of good options as Kathy did (Kathy's story follows on page 61) or you may have very few. Know which types of coverage you are eligible for and how the various products within those categories compare. Remember that sometimes within a family, it may make sense for one spouse to stay on COBRA while another spouse and children pursue other options.

Coverage option alternatives and information to help evaluate options follow on pages 59 and 60. Remember, if a type of insurance is "medically underwritten," the insurer has broad discretion to deny your application. If the insurance is "guaranteed issue," then as long as you meet the qualifications for the coverage, you have a right to the coverage.

As you can see, many coverage options in the United States are guaranteed issue BUT you must be eligible for the coverage and able to afford it especially if you are paying yourself.

A more detailed definition of each option, when to consider that option and how to learn about the options available in your state are included in the Appendix.

Other options like Medicaid, limited benefit Plans, other government programs, etc., are also briefly defined in the Appendix but consideration of them is beyond the scope of this work.

TYPICAL COVERAGE OPTIONS
WHEN LOSING GROUP COVERAGE

TYPE OF COVERAGE	DEFINITION
COBRA	Temporary extension of group coverage at your expense
Individual Insurance	Insurance you apply for and buy; in most (but not all) states it is medically underwritten so the insurer can deny application
Sole Proprietor	Insurance you buy as a self-employed person; guaranteed issue
Association	Insurance you buy through membership in an organization; Plans vary but usually such coverage is not medically underwritten
Small Group	Insurance a small business of at least two owners or an owner and an employee; guaranteed issue
Large Group	Insurance typically subsidized through a large employer or union; guaranteed issue
State High Risk Pool	State program for HIPAA-eligible people and/or those who have not been able to buy insurance as an individual; guaranteed issue
Conversion	State program for HIPAA-eligible people and/or those who have not been able to buy insurance as an individual; guaranteed issue
Temporary Pre-existing Condition High Risk Pool	Program created by reform legislation for those with pre-existing conditions and no insurance coverage for at least six months; guaranteed issue
Medicare	Coverage through the federal government for which most Americans are eligible at age 65 because they paid into Social Security long enough or were married to someone who did; guaranteed issue (but strict enrollment rules)

EVALUATING (NON-MEDICARE) COVERAGE
OPTIONS AFTER LOSING GROUP COVERAGE
(Simplified for illustration purposes)

OPTION	AVAILABLE	AFFORDABLE**	LONG-TERM	OTHER
On parent's Plan	To age 26 if coverage not available to you through your work.	Perhaps–group coverage often subsidized.	No–but some states have higher age limits.	Small business may not subsidize dependents.
On spouse's Plan	If spouse on active group Plan, your loss is "qualifying event."	Perhaps–group coverage often subsidized.	Depends on job security of spouse.	Small business may not subsidize dependents.
COBRA	Almost always if group provides coverage and continues to exist.	Depends on group rates and your finances.	NEVER–but route to HIPAA conversion option.	May not be option for survivors of sole proprietor Plan.
Individual insurance*	Guaranteed in five states; in others must be healthy to qualify.	Depends on state and often your age and health.	Yes–if you stay in service area and insurer remains in business.	Some Plans are portable.
State High Risk Pool*	In 34 states. May need to exhaust COBRA or be denied individual insurance.	Typically costly. Premiums usually based on age.	Yes–if you don't move to another state.	Some Plans have reciprocity with other states.
Conversion*	In 11 states. May need to exhaust COBRA or be denied individual insurance.	Typically costly. Premiums usually based on age.	Yes–if you don't move to another state.	State options vary widely. Investigate.
Association	Have to be eligible.	Depends on rates and your finances.	Yes–if you remain eligible.	Some poor options in this category. Review carefully.
Sole Proprietor	Have to be eligible.	Yes–if business prospers.	Yes–if you remain eligible.	State options vary widely. Review carefully.
Small Group	If you own and run small business with other owner or employee.	Yes–if business prospers.	Yes–if business prospers.	Insurers don't have uniform definition but usually two or more covered lives.

*If ACA is upheld and 2014 provisions implemented, these options will likely be consolidated by state.

**A relative term. Comprehensive coverage in the U.S. is costly.

The discussion that follows addresses a variety of situations and events associated with a healthcare coverage transition. I have included separate sections on "electing COBRA" and "exhausting COBRA" even though COBRA is triggered by many of the events which follow like job loss, divorce, retirement or death of a spouse.

As stated before, don't limit yourself only to the section that deals with the type of transition you face. The more you read about coverage transitions, the more you'll appreciate the strategic thinking involved in developing a good Coverage Plan.

Elect COBRA?

Kathy was in the process of getting divorced. She knew she had a right to COBRA coverage for 36 months after the divorce was final. As a healthy woman in her late 30s, she also would qualify for individual coverage which was medically underwritten in her state. Kathy was a talented artist and was planning to open a gallery in order to show and sell her artwork. In her state, that meant Kathy could qualify for coverage as a sole proprietor and if she hired an employee who worked the required number of hours and provided coverage for that employee, then Kathy could obtain small group coverage.

We helped Kathy weigh the advantages and disadvantages of all these options. COBRA was the most comprehensive medical option and included dental but also the most expensive option. The individual coverage was the least expensive option because Kathy was relatively young and premiums are based on age in her state. The individual coverage didn't have benefits like maternity but Kathy wasn't concerned about maternity benefits. She already had two children and wasn't planning on having any more. The sole proprietor coverage seemed the least attractive option as it was more expensive than individual coverage but had a very limited drug benefit.

The other thing Kathy had to weigh was the fact that should she take COBRA and develop a pre-existing condition while on COBRA, she would not be eligible for the generally affordable cost of individual, private coverage due to her health. In such a situation, Kathy would still be eligible for the High Risk Pool Program in her state because she would have been HIPAA-eligible, but that was an even more expensive option than COBRA.

Kathy decided on individual coverage and was approved. Fifteen months later she was diagnosed with breast cancer so in her case, she'd made the lucky choice. She was the policy holder of her individual coverage through the local Blue Cross and Blue Shield Plan and although her rates will continue to increase, her coverage can't be taken away as long as she pays her premiums.

EXHAUSTING COBRA

As mentioned previously, if you've chosen COBRA and your COBRA is ending, you are a HIPAA-eligible person and every state has a guaranteed issue option for you to get healthcare coverage. This is misunderstood but true. Unfortunately, COBRA is often expensive and the options when COBRA is exhausted can be even more costly. It depends on the individual situation.

In evaluating coverage options when COBRA is ending, you should ask the following questions:

+ If you live in one of 45 states where private, individual insurance is medically underwritten: Do I have what an insurer would consider a pre-existing condition? Have I had significant medical expenses recently? Am I on any expensive medications, etc.?
+ How comprehensive should my coverage and provider network be?
+ What can I afford?
+ Am I looking for a long-term or short-term option?
+ Can I freelance? Are their coverage options for freelancers in my area?
+ Do I have or can I start a small business?

Divorced Woman with COBRA and Pre-existing Conditions

As the following case example illustrates, those who are in a position to start a business and qualify for small group coverage often have more coverage options and options they control. Many people who lose their jobs, particularly professionals who can consult or have some other special expertise, should think strategically about their ability to start a business and obtain group coverage through the business, even if they continue to look for a job.

When Sandy's COBRA coverage was ending as a result of her divorce we met with her to discuss options. She had had a successful bout with cancer but it was too recent an experience to think she could qualify for coverage in the private, individual marketplace. In all, her COBRA premium was at the low end but the premium for her state's High Risk Pool Program was extremely expensive for her and funds were an issue.

I asked her several times if she had any plans to return to work or start a business of some sort or do freelance work which might lead to another path for coverage. As the meeting neared an end, I asked one last time if there might be any other way in her future she could see qualifying for coverage other than the High Risk Pool. She sheepishly admitted that she had started a catering business with a friend but that her only clients had been neighbors so it didn't seem like a going concern to her.

I asked,

"Have you and your partner established an LLC?"

"Do you have documented revenue?"

"Do you have a business checking account?"

> *A small business can be*
> *a very desirable vehicle for obtaining*
> *healthcare coverage.*

She answered yes to every question. I asked if she was committed to building the business, that it wasn't simply a hobby. "Of course," she answered. Sandy still wasn't sure this business would qualify her for group coverage because her partner had coverage through her husband. I explained that what she described to me was a legitimate group of two with one waiving out of coverage and there would likely be options. Sandy was able to obtain group coverage with no pre-existing condition issues as a result of HIPAA laws since her COBRA was ending and she would transition to group coverage within 63 days.

TURNING 26

Under ACA, most Plans must allow adult children to remain on a parent's Plan to age 26 unless they are eligible for group coverage through their work.

When a 26 year old ages off a parent's Plan, he will have a right to COBRA and, once exhausting COBRA, guaranteed coverage of some sort by being HIPAA-eligible. Since COBRA is often unaffordable, these are the questions the 25 year old losing coverage at 26 needs to consider when planning:

+ How much will COBRA cost? Can I afford it?
+ Does either parent have coverage that allows an adult child to stay on beyond age 26?
+ Am I looking for a long-term or short-term option? Is short term insurance available in my state?
+ Am I likely to be offered employer or union sponsored coverage soon through an existing or new job?
+ Do I have what an insurer would consider a pre-existing condition (if in one of the 45 states where private, individual insurance is medically underwritten)?
+ Is coverage in my state "guaranteed issue" (based on residence not health status)?
+ How comprehensive should the coverage be? Should I consider a high deductible Plan?
+ Can I freelance? Do I have or can I start a legitimate small business?
+ Am I making so little income that I can qualify for protection through a state program of some sort?

Many individual insurance products in the private marketplace do not include maternity coverage so a young woman has to be mindful of what she will do should she get pregnant while on that type of coverage.

Sometimes a High Risk Pool option isn't that unattractive for a relatively young person because the rates are typically based on age. We recently even recommended that a young healthy spouse go on a High Risk Pool Plan as her husband is already on the Plan. She is a young woman who was planning a pregnancy. She is not eligible for group coverage and her husband is a graduate student who isn't eligible for group coverage either. Coverage options as the spouse of a student or in the individual insurance marketplace had waiting periods, limited obstetrical networks or both. Normally you would not consider a High Risk Pool option for a healthy individual but this was clearly her best option and the lesson is to consider all options.

The most attractive solution for the younger person (and almost anyone else for that matter) is almost always to find a job with benefits. Many can't find a job with benefits. Others have a job that doesn't offer benefits because the business owner either can't or feels he or she can't afford to provide health insurance. If you're on your own do your homework on options and get sound advice.

DIVORCE

A particularly cruel aspect of the fact that most coverage in our country is tied to a job is that it affects so many women who lose their coverage as a result of divorce. Of course, if you are getting divorced and have coverage through your own employment, divorce does not affect your coverage. But women getting divorced are often a dependent on their spouse's Plan. Sometimes men are, too. Even if they are relatively healthy, women getting divorced are more likely to be in counseling, taking prescription medicine for depression or both which typically makes them ineligible for private, individual insurance which is medically underwritten. Many women are shocked to find that in addition to their family breaking up and the loss of financial support, they are losing their subsidized group coverage.

So often with divorce, it seems both parties lose financially, so the added responsibility of paying for one's own health insurance feels even more burdensome. This group often suffers "sticker shock" after they learn the cost of COBRA coverage.

I have spoken widely on Healthcare Coverage and Divorce and was even invited to speak in Canada where divorce does not affect healthcare coverage. Through these conferences as well as other experiences, I learned that many former husbands have offered to keep their ex-wives on their Plans as spouses. At times I've even been told this was a divorce attorney's recommendation. This is a very bad idea. The term "eligibility" was discussed earlier.

You have to be eligible for coverage for an insurer to have an obligation to pay your claims. Knowingly remaining on an insurance Plan when you are not an eligible dependent is viewed by the insurance company as insurance fraud. The insurer may accept the premium payments and may not "catch" you but if you have large claims and they discover you are not an eligible dependent, they have a right to deny those claims.

We had one client whose former husband had remarried and she thought she could still be on his Plan. You should always be ELIGIBLE for your coverage so no insurer can deny your claims.

We've also seen this problem with former husbands who own businesses and add their ex-wives and/or adult children as employees even when they're not. To some this seems smart but it's extremely foolish. From an insurer's perspective and any state insurance department regulator, these practices are insurance fraud.

In dealing with the options for divorced women, state of residence matters. In New York where individual premiums are prohibitively expensive, almost everyone with a COBRA right will choose it over individual insurance if they are not working. But again, COBRA is often expensive and always temporary so even for three years, you should consider COBRA a short-term option. In states where individual insurance is medically underwritten, the largest problem divorced women have is qualifying for the coverage because so often they are in counseling or taking prescription drugs for anxiety or depression.

> *A divorced spouse can **never** be an eligible dependent on a former spouse's plan.*

Woman Took Valium:
Insurance Denied

Joan was in her late 50s and getting divorced. She had been an at-home Mom for many years and after her children grew up, she worked as a volunteer for several local charitable agencies. Joan had not worked on a paid basis since early in her marriage and felt the prospect of gaining employment in a setting with good health-care coverage was unlikely. COBRA seemed very expensive so she applied for individual coverage and was denied. In her Health Questionnaire, a form similar to what one fills out as a new patient in a doctor's office, she had answered all the questions related to various ailments as "No." However, she was taking valium for anxiety and that was enough for the insurer to deny her application. Joan opted for COBRA.

At the end of COBRA, Joan re-applied for individual insurance and was denied a second time because she was still taking valium. Joan's only option for coverage was the state's High Risk Pool Program. Joan obtained that coverage but it was very expensive. Joan felt she had to try to taper off the valium and did so over a six-month period. Unfortunately an application for individual insurance will ask the question, "have you ever been denied coverage?" and Joan had been denied twice. Joan reapplied a third time for private, individual coverage addressing the valium issue head-on with a letter from her doctor validating that she was doing well and had been off the valium for months. Joan was approved.

Paid COBRA Premium Late

Rita had been on COBRA for two years after her divorce. One January she made two payments and several weeks later received a letter stating, "the coverage described below has been cancelled upon request and can't be reinstated." Rita had never requested cancellation of her coverage. Rita called the Service Center, was told she'd have to appeal, filed an appeal and several months later received a letter stating her coverage would be reinstated but the coverage wasn't reinstated.

At this point knowing her COBRA would have been ending soon anyway, Rita applied for coverage to Golden Rule in Florida. She was denied private, individual coverage due to pre-existing conditions but was told that she did have access to a HIPAA Portability Plan if she could produce a HIPAA certificate from the prior insurer showing she had not had a break in coverage of greater than 63 days. That is when Rita came to us for assistance. She needed to have her former coverage reinstated in order to have a coverage transition after COBRA was exhausted.

Throughout this ordeal, we learned how brutally aggressive the COBRA administrator for this large national bank had been. The letter sent to Rita suggesting she had requested cancellation of her coverage was a mistake. As we learned more about the situation, it appeared that Rita had been terminated either because of one inadvertent underpayment of $6.18 or because she paid January's premium in January and the company said the payment was due in December.

The company's representatives consistently referred us to the COBRA administrator and those working for the COBRA administrator maintained they had no authority to resolve the situation. In the end we did prevail and Rita's COBRA was reinstated retroactively, she paid all her back premiums and she was able to get a letter of creditable coverage showing she hadn't had a gap in 63 days so could go on the Portability Plan. We were very persistent.

Missing COBRA Notice

Evelyn had just gotten divorced. She and her husband owned two homes and as part of the settlement, she was to prepare their second home to be sold. She was away for several weeks at the second home and did not have her mail forwarded. When she returned to her primary residence she realized her COBRA notice had arrived while she was away and she immediately sent a letter to the employer asking for consideration. The response she received was harsh and clearly stated that no exceptions would be made for missing the COBRA notice deadline.

Your letter indicates you missed making your payment…. It is the COBRA participant's responsibility to pay the monthly premiums in a timely fashion, whether an invoice is received or not.

If a premium is not received by the required deadline, benefits are terminated retroactively to the last day of the month in which a full premium payment was received. Because your COBRA payment was not received by the required deadline, we are unable to reinstate your coverage.

During this period we told Evelyn she needed to apply to New York's Direct Pay Plan (individual insurance provided on guaranteed issue basis) to have insurance in place. Since this is a guaranteed issue program she was accepted. However, the premium for Evelyn's Empire coverage is $1,611.00 per month versus the $512.00 per month her COBRA coverage would have cost. Having the Empire coverage rather than COBRA coverage for three years will cost Evelyn about $40,000.00 more in insurance premiums. Hers was a costly oversight. Worse, several months later Evelyn was told she should have a surgical procedure which the insurer said it would deny based on its right to impose a pre-existing condition exclusion for 12 months since Evelyn had had a break in coverage one month longer than the 63 day HIPAA timeframe.

Evelyn was treated very harshly at an extremely vulnerable period in her life. Sadly, that's why people must be extremely conscientious in dealing with health insurance matters.

INVOLUNTARY JOB LOSS

Job loss occurs under many different types of circumstances. We can be fired, laid-off, retire or opt to leave an employer. Some sell a business. In almost all situations where an individual had group coverage, the departing person has a right to COBRA coverage.

The coverage implications associated with leaving a job depend largely on whether the departure was planned, whether there are dependents, the best option for each dependent and whether the worker and/or spouse was over or under age 65.

If you are leaving one position and already have a job secured, please also go to the section on Group Coverage Traps and Gaps and if you are retiring or dealing with a spouse's retirement, please go to the retirement section of the book. This section is largely written for the person who has involuntarily lost his job and faces loss of healthcare coverage.

A lay-off or reduction in force is often accompanied by severance that includes a period of employer-subsidized coverage before the opportunity to elect COBRA. Taking that coverage is a straightforward matter for someone under age 65. Severance issues are more complicated for the person who worked for a large employer and is eligible for Medicare or has a spouse eligible for Medicare. If you fall into that category, please read the case study in the Missing Medicare Part B Special Enrollment Period in the Medicare section of the book.

HUSBAND AND WIFE BOTH EMPLOYED

When a husband and wife are both employed through businesses that offer healthcare coverage, the family will typically be covered under one spouse's Plan. When healthcare coverage didn't cost so much, many dually employed couples maintained both sources of coverage on each other's Plans but that's not common today.

Should the spouse with the coverage lose his or her position, that job loss is a qualifying event and will still allow the couple or family to get on the other spouse's coverage "off-cycle" or outside the Annual Enrollment Period. Group coverage is almost always the best option since employer or union provided coverage is typically paying for most of the cost of coverage.

For a household with one worker, COBRA is often unaffordable. But try not to skimp on something as vital as coverage. COBRA can be an excellent option if the following apply:

+ COBRA is a temporary bridge to another job

- COBRA will enable you reach age 65 when you are eligible for Medicare
- You have a pre-existing condition and have no option for private individual coverage in your state because you likely won't be accepted
- You live in a "guaranteed issue" state and COBRA is less costly than alternatives
- You have no other options as a sole proprietor or small business owner
- You were on a spouse's Plan, your spouse died and you need time to plan
- Cost of premiums is not a consideration and you plan to exhaust COBRA and go onto the HIPAA-required conversion option in your state

But, you need to consider the options and their advantages and disadvantages for **every family member** both short-term and long-term. If you have children who can be covered under a state-subsidized program because you have no income, find out what's available to them.

If you can take COBRA to age 65 (Medicare eligibility), it is often an attractive alternative to other options charging higher rates based on age.

Involuntary Job Loss

Elaine lost her job at age 27. COBRA was almost $700.00/month. She was in New York where individual insurance premiums even for an HMO were higher than COBRA. She looked at various association options there, like the Freelancers Union, but she didn't qualify for their coverage. She was totally healthy and totally exasperated. She decided to move back to her parents' home in Connecticut to be eligible for inexpensive individual insurance coverage there.

Joe lost his job in his early 60s. He had pre-existing conditions so took COBRA. However, he had a younger wife and she qualified for individual insurance at a much lower rate. Joe hoped to be re-employed before his 18 months of COBRA ran out. He didn't have a post-COBRA Plan yet but knew he had a deadline if he couldn't find another job quickly.

Jean was in her late 50s and worked for a large employer so her older husband, Jack, was eligible for her group Plan as a dependent and avoided paying Medicare Part B and Part D premiums. When she was laid off, he decided to go on Medicare B and D and a private Supplement. Jean's COBRA rates were cheaper than insurance in the individual private marketplace. That surprised Jean but her employer was a large private company with many young, healthy workers so rates were pretty reasonable. She decided to take COBRA since the rate was unusually attractive knowing that if she developed a pre-existing condition while on COBRA, she wouldn't be able to qualify for individual insurance. She was considering starting a new business anyway which she knew could be a vehicle for coverage.

Lynn lost her job with a large company. They provided her with severance and an extension of her group coverage and then she took COBRA. By the end of COBRA she had started her own consulting firm and also sat on several corporate Boards. Sole proprietor coverage in her state was a better option than private individual insurance and small group insurance wasn't an option since she was self-employed and had no other employees. She applied and was approved.

Some people will have few options for coverage but others will have several as well as several options for family members. Be strategic when it comes to planning and get good advice.

RETIREMENT OR RETIREMENT OF A SPOUSE

Sometimes we plan our retirement; other times it is foisted upon us. But if you're fortunate enough to be encouraged to retire from a large company and you are eligible for retiree medical, you may be one of the lucky few, as far as coverage is concerned, if the coverage is good and the cost to you reasonable. If you are under age 65, however, you should determine if the retiree medical ends at age 65 or extends beyond age 65. If you are 65 or over and have a spouse on the Plan, you must know if there are survivor benefits should you predecease your spouse.

We often see the dwindling value of retiree medical benefits, particularly for retirees 65 and over for whom Medicare is primary. Let me quote from one of our client's Retiree Benefits Booklets:

> (*The company*) *reserves the right any time, at its discretion, to amend, modify, reduce or terminate any of the retiree health and welfare programs described or referenced in this brochure. This may be done at any time, including after retirement, the onset of disability or death.*

This is not very warm language from a company you may have spent decades or perhaps your entire adult life committed to. Employers are under tremendous pressure, however, due to the rising costs of healthcare. Most are preserving their rights to modify, reduce and even eliminate benefits.

If you have retiree coverage through a former employer, always determine whether it ends at 65 or is a lifetime benefit.

If retirement does not include retiree medical, many of the issues and options discussed in Involuntary Job Loss above are similar. Any reader under 65 should review the Involuntary Job Loss section of this book. Those about to turn 65 or over 65 should read the entire Medicare section.

Retirement seems like a process that should be well planned but we see many thoughtful people and others who haven't planned well or haven't planned at all. They may not have dealt with obtaining coverage on their own before so underestimate the difficulty or cost of a transition. Often, a sudden decline in health by one spouse takes the couple by surprise. At a certain age, it's time to give some thought to the issue of how you'll have coverage after leaving the workforce.

As with every other transition, you must know what your options are especially if you or a family member have a pre-existing condition which might lead to your not being eligible for coverage in the individual private insurance marketplace. Taking COBRA is almost always an option for someone planning to retire and if you are within 18 months of turning 65, that's a pretty sure plan for transitioning from the group coverage onto Medicare.

Of course, as we get older we are more apt to have medical issues that an insurer would consider a pre-existing condition that would prevent us from getting coverage from them. Five retirement stories illustrating various traps and gaps are presented on pages following.

Diligent and Thoughtful Planning

Donald was 70 years old and had served as the CEO for a small company (but over 20 employees) for many years and was thinking about retiring soon. He hoped he could negotiate an arrangement where he could stay on the Group Plan. His wife Catherine was in her 50s and also on Donald's company's Plan although she worked for a small company through which she could get coverage. They didn't believe her Plan was nearly as good as Donald's Plan due to both benefits and the provider network and hoped they could also arrange something where she could remain on Donald's insurance after he retired. There was also a concern about her past medical history that an insurer might consider a pre-existing condition.

First, we explained to Donald and Catherine that since this was a small company with no retiree benefits, a special arrangement negotiated for them to remain on the group Plan after he retired didn't seem a viable option. This gets back to the concept of eligibility. Once Donald retires from his company, a company that has no retiree program and no plans to establish one, Donald would be eligible to continue his group benefits temporarily through COBRA but cannot remain an active part of the employee health Plan.

A small employer like Donald's would have a fully insured health Plan regulated under state law. Eligibility requirements vary from state to state, for example, how many hours one might have to work to be eligible for the employer's coverage, but you are not eligible nor could your spouse be eligible for benefits except through a COBRA extension.

Donald was also hoping he could avoid going on Medicare since he had heard that some doctors were deciding not to take Medicare at all or not take new Medicare patients. We explained to Donald that enrolling in Medicare Part B was not required by the government but practically speaking there simply aren't other attractive coverage options once one is retired and eligible for Medicare. Also, Medicare enrollment rules are punitive when you don't sign up for Medicare according to government rules designed to prevent people from enrolling just when they get sick.

After a number of discussions, Donald understood that upon retirement, he should enroll in Medicare Part B (he already had A) and go on Medicare and its related products and programs including a private Supplement and Part D coverage for prescription drugs.

Meanwhile we were working on Catherine's options. There were a number of them:

Donald's retirement would create a qualifying event for her even if he didn't take COBRA so she would be eligible to take COBRA, a temporary extension of group benefits.

Donald's retirement would also create a qualifying event for Catherine which would allow her to enroll in her company's Plan off-cycle from the Annual Open Enrollment Period.

And what if Catherine wanted to retire? She was many years away from Medicare eligibility.

Catherine could apply for individual coverage in her state of residence, South Carolina. Premiums are age-rated (the older you are the more you pay) in South Carolina and pre-existing conditions would be taken into account until at least to 2014, if reform is implemented as passed.

> *Thoughtful Coverage Planning is a must when one ages onto Medicare years ahead of a younger spouse. The couple will have very different coverage options.*

If Catherine were denied individual coverage, there was also a High Risk Pool Program available in South Carolina. This would be an expensive source of coverage but Catherine was reassured knowing that whatever Donald planned related to his retirement and whatever she planned related to hers, should she not qualify for individual insurance in the private marketplace she would still have a good, comprehensive option for coverage. They were relieved.

Remorseful Retiree Botches Wife's Health Coverage after his Retirement

A spouse's retirement can be enormously problematic especially in those situations where the man is the policy holder, the wife is younger and/or there are young children. Retiree medical benefits through a company or union are a source of protection in this situation but fewer and fewer people are getting retiree medical benefits.

> Michael had worked for a large company in a senior position for decades but the company did not offer any retiree medical. He decided to retire when he was 63 and he and his wife, Mary, took COBRA for 18 months. He sought our advice to help with the transition onto Medicare. We also discussed his wife's situation. She was five years younger than Michael. She was able to extend her COBRA beyond the initial 18 months, to a total of 36 months, when Michael went on Medicare. However, she had several health issues which a private insurance Plan would have considered a pre-existing

condition. Her only realistic option for coverage when her COBRA finally ended was the state's High Risk Pool Program which was exceedingly expensive for someone in her 60s. Having had good group coverage his entire life, Michael had no idea Mary's coverage could be so expensive through the High Risk Pool (December 2011 rates for the Plan she was on were $1,588.12 per month). In retrospect, he wished he had remained employed rather than retire when he did.

Got Coverage through Trusted Professional Association and Paid Dearly

Husband and wife physicians in their 50s decided to retire. The wife had a brief scare due to a breast cancer diagnosis but the breast cancer was caught early, she was treated and she was fine. They were correct to think any recent breast cancer diagnosis would make it unlikely that she could qualify for private individual insurance that is medically underwritten. Instead, they both obtained coverage through a surgical association which imposed very hefty premium increases over the years. When their premiums exceeded $40,000.00 per person per year, they wanted to consider other options. The husband was able to obtain high deductible individual insurance with the state's Blue Cross and Blue Shield Plan at a cost of about $6,000.00/year. The wife was able to obtain good coverage through the state's High Risk Pool Program. She chose a high deductible Plan and also had premiums of about $6,000.00/year. Both of them established health savings accounts as part of their new coverage which helped them pay expenses with pre-tax dollars before their deductibles were met.

Broker Gives Retiree
Incorrect Information

When Joe retired after a long career with a large company, he and his wife, Peggy, both had excellent retiree medical benefits. He was told there were no survivor benefits for his wife should he predecease her. Joe met with a broker who told him he should buy a Medicare Supplement for his wife because otherwise she might not be able to buy a Supplement if he predeceased her and if she had developed a pre-existing condition. This information was wrong. First, should Joe predecease his wife she would have a COBRA right to extend the retiree coverage because she would be a HIPAA-eligible person and already on Medicare A and B. She also would have a guaranteed right to purchase a Medicare Supplement within 63 days as a HIPAA-eligible person losing group coverage. Second, she lived in a state where Supplements that didn't impose a waiting period for pre-existing conditions were available. Joe paid for the Supplement for his wife for many years even though it duplicated the coverage she already had through his former employer.

Misses Medicare Special Enrollment
after Wife's Retirement

George was covered through his younger wife's large group employer. When she was an active employee, he didn't need to enroll in Medicare Part B. She retired and neither of them focused on the fact that her Plan required anyone 65 or over to have Medicare Parts A and B as primary. George missed his Part B Special Enrollment Period. Of course, he was able to enroll in Medicare during the General Enrollment Period during the first quarter of each year but he will pay premium penalties for life and in the meantime he had a frightening gap in coverage and he had a history of cardiovascular disease.

DEATH OF A SPOUSE

A coverage transition associated with the death of a spouse is also an immensely cruel part of our largely employer-based approach to coverage. I have seen a good number of condolence letters to, mostly, the new widow. As mentioned before, the closing line is often "you may elect COBRA during your COBRA election period but you will be terminated from the Group Health Plan at the end of the month." In order to maintain continuous coverage, electing COBRA is often the only desirable, practical decision immediately following a spouse's death. My plea would be for the surviving spouse to carefully evaluate coverage options just as soon as possible.

Like all other transitions, death of a spouse can result in a number of different coverage options depending on the situation. In the opening chapters of the book, we discussed the Watson family where a sole proprietor's death resulted in immediate termination of coverage. The insurer initially opposed extending coverage for even a month. To lose your husband and father suddenly and prematurely is a tragedy. Adding to it the loss of the protection healthcare coverage provides with no notice is unspeakably inhumane.

When both a husband and wife have coverage through their respective jobs, death of a spouse will not affect the other's coverage. In Lynn's case described on page 81, however, staying on her own Plan almost resulted in forfeiting her right to retiree medical lifetime survivor benefits. There is a substantial risk with dually employed couples that the employer will not extend retiree medical benefits to a spouse who was not on the Plan at the time of the subscriber's death. Hence, best to have a Coverage Plan.

INDIVIDUAL INSURANCE

If husband and wife each have individual insurance, the death of one spouse doesn't affect the other's health insurance because each was deemed eligible for the coverage at the time it was granted.

MEDICARE

If a husband and wife have Medicare as their primary insurance when one of them dies, coverage is not as totally disrupted as it is for younger couples. When a surviving spouse is already on Medicare as primary, at least Medicare Parts A and B are in place. Medicare Supplements, Medicare Part D Plans and Medicare Advantage Plans are provided to **individuals**. There is no relationship to a group. If one spouse dies the coverage of the other spouse is not affected.

> *If a Retiree Medical Plan doesn't have survivor benefits and the retired employee predeceases his or her spouse, that spouse will have a right to COBRA.*

If the secondary coverage, however, is retiree medical through a former employer, **one needs to know if there are survivor benefits.** A widow with no survivor benefits must consider her options. One may only have 63 days, the HIPAA period, to transition, if necessary, to a Medicare Supplement and Part D Plan. COBRA is not typically an attractive option for someone on Medicare because COBRA is expensive and the combination of Medicare primary and COBRA secondary is expensive, cumbersome and temporary. Even though the secondary coverage may not change if there are survivor benefits, the transition must be managed because the surviving spouse who was a dependent may now be considered the subscriber by the insurer and will often be given a new insurance card with a new number.

A wife who did not earn Medicare on her own Social Security record will get a new Medicare card with a different suffix after her husband's death. This does not change her Medicare benefits and should not affect Medicare claims.

From COBRA to Individual Coverage

Victoria was in her late 50s when her husband died and she and her college student son elected COBRA for three years. At the end of the COBRA period both were in good health and their advisor had shopped on-line for individual two-person coverage with Victoria being the subscriber. Since health insurance in their state was age-rated, applying for two-person coverage with Virginia as the subscriber would have cost Victoria an extra $4,000.00 or so a year because the son could qualify for an individual policy on his own at a vastly lower rate based on his age than she could in her early

60s. They each applied separately for individual coverage and were approved.

Medicare Eligible

Mary's husband worked for a large company and she was on his Plan as a dependent. She enrolled in Medicare Part A but the company Plan was primary for all services and she had no reason to enroll in Medicare Part B. When her husband died suddenly she received a letter of condolence reminding her that her active group coverage would terminate at the end of the month although she could elect COBRA. Her husband's company did not offer retiree medical and hence there were no survivor benefits either. Mary decided to immediately enroll in Medicare Part B because the loss of group coverage created a Part B Special Enrollment Period. A Medicare Part B Special Enrollment Period, much like being "HIPAA-eligible," also allowed Mary a guaranteed right to enroll in a Medicare Supplement and a Part D prescription drug Plan as long as she acted within 63 days.

Widow Not on Husband's Plan Deemed Ineligible for Lifetime Retiree Medical

Lynn's husband had been a senior executive with one company for his entire career. Lynn was also working and had coverage of her own through work. Lynn's husband was diagnosed with cancer and had a rapid decline and died. Of course, since Lynn wasn't on his Plan, her husband's death didn't affect her coverage. Two years later, Lynn started to plan her retirement but 18 months of COBRA wasn't going to take her to age 65 and Medicare eligibility. She sought our assistance.

Our research determined that Lynn's husband's Plan, through a large, national bank, had provided for lifetime survivor benefits. However, the company's position was that she was ineligible because she had to be on the company's Plan at the time of his death and she was not. This seemed particularly illogical to Lynn since having maintained her own coverage for many years she had actually saved her husband's company from having to pay for any medical services for her. Lynn probably wouldn't have had any luck gaining access to the company Plan had she been forced to go through regular channels. Fortunately, her husband had been a fairly high-level executive with the bank so a friend of his at the company intervened on her behalf. In the end, a settlement was agreed to where the company let Lynn pay premiums retroactively to the month of her husband's death so that she could be considered on the Plan at that time and therefore eligible for her lifetime retiree medical benefits.

> *To be eligible for retiree medical benefits as a survivor, you may need to be on the Plan at the time of your spouse's death, instead of your own Plan if you have coverage through your employer.*

Survivor Benefits
and Excellent Retiree Medical

Eleanor's husband died after a brief illness. They both had Medicare Parts A and B and excellent retiree coverage with survivor benefits through his former employer. Eleanor had to work through the Benefits Administrator so that she could become the subscriber rather than a dependent on her deceased husband's Plan. The coverage was so good there was no reason to consider other options. Eleanor also received a new Medicare card with her husband's social with a "D" rather than a "B" on the end. Receiving a new Medicare card with a new suffix alarmed Eleanor at first. We explained that her Medicare benefits were unchanged. The "D" suffix indicates to Social Security that she continues to be entitled to Social Security and Medicare benefits through a deceased rather than living spouse.

Every year Eleanor receives a letter of creditable coverage from her deceased husband's former employer indicating her drug coverage is as good as or better than Medicare Part D. Eleanor saves that letter just in case the retiree coverage should ever be eliminated and she needs to enroll in Medicare Part D without premium penalties.

MOVING

In general, your health insurance should align with your state of residence. If you have group coverage, your employer normally manages this issue but look at what happened to Mr. and Mrs. Stevens with his promotion! Leave nothing to chance. Find out how a relocation or promotion will affect your coverage before you accept.

If you have individual coverage or even a Medicare Supplement or Part D Plan, you need to understand the coverage implications when you move to another state. Moving can have a negative impact, a neutral impact or can provide better options than you had in your previous state. It all depends on your situation. Joanne Yamamoto's move from California to North Carolina helped her obtain better coverage.

We are seeing more people moving out of their home countries for estate planning purposes without factoring healthcare coverage into their Plan. **Please know that U.S. insurers will likely not accept coverage from outside the U.S. as "creditable."**

California Resident Moves to State with Sole Proprietor Coverage

Claire was a massage therapist in northern California and her coverage was through conversion of a prior policy she had had through North Carolina Blue Cross and Blue Shield. When she moved out of California and back to North Carolina, she applied to another company for individual coverage. She was granted the coverage but had a 12-month waiting period imposed for the one medication she took for anxiety as well as any mental health services. These were the only services of importance to her at the time. Unfortunately, Claire had terminated her prior individual coverage which had included the rare conversion option. Fortunately, North Carolina had sole proprietor coverage or essentially coverage for a self-employed individual. As a group of one, Claire's coverage was based on her eligibility as a sole proprietor rather than her health status. She applied for and was granted that coverage with no pre-existing condition issues or waiting periods.

Woman with Individual Coverage: Company allows Conversion to New State

Sarah, a woman in her mid-50s was married to an older man already on Medicare. They wanted to make their Florida home their permanent residence. Were they to relocate and have her apply for individual coverage in Florida, Sarah would not have been accepted due to pre-existing conditions. However, Sarah had a Blue Cross/Blue Shield policy which entitled her to convert her existing Kentucky policy to a Florida Plan. It was very wise of her to have chosen the Kentucky Plan that she did. Otherwise as an individual with no HIPAA rights, she would not have been able to qualify for individual insurance in Florida.

Coverage through State High Risk Pool

Margie had a history of eating disorders that she had largely overcome. Nevertheless these past problems prevented her from obtaining coverage in the individual private insurance marketplace in her home state of Connecticut. As a result, she applied for and obtained coverage through the Connecticut Health Reinsurance Association, Connecticut's High Risk Pool Program. She later decided to move to California. California also has a High Risk Pool Program. Margie contacted the California Major Risk Medical Insurance Program and learned there was no reciprocity between the two high risk programs.

In order to apply for coverage through California's Program, Margie needed to establish residency in California and prove that she had been denied coverage by a private insurance company within two years. Margie had not saved proof of her denial from the first insurer she had approached which led her to apply to the Connecticut Health Reinsurance Association. Margie applied again to the Connecticut insurer which issued the original denial and her application was denied again. This written denial enabled her to complete the California Program's application. Margie was extremely anxious because the information she had received from the California Program stated that they maintained a waiting list and she did not want to be without coverage. Margie was fortunate. She was accepted by the California Program and coverage started on the first of the following month.

Coverage through a state's High Risk Pool Program is always tied to your state of residence. Reciprocity agreements between states are rare. Plan carefully before moving to another state or you could lose healthcare coverage.

Couple with Individual Coverage Move to New State

John and Sally bought individual coverage in Arizona where they had lived for a number of years. Although they kept their home in Arizona, over time they actually became legal residents of Nevada. In the fine print of their Arizona policy was wording that the coverage applied only to legal residents of Arizona. When they came to us for help we suggested that their coverage should align with their state of residence. To maintain coverage from a Plan that requires you to live in the state when it is not your official domicile risks a dispute over eligibility and claims. Fortunately John and Sally were healthy individuals who were easily able to obtain individual coverage in Nevada by applying on-line to a reputable Plan. In fact, the new coverage was far superior to what they had in place in Arizona.

Adult Studying Abroad with Family

Martin was getting a doctorate degree in England. He, his wife and young children were covered by the British Healthcare System during that period. While they were outside the U.S., Martin's wife, Debby, was diagnosed with diabetes. They had maintained an individual policy written in the U.S. but it was very poor coverage, had no drug coverage at all and was not considered creditable. On their move back to the U.S., they learned that even in the states where Sandy could get onto a State High Risk Pool Plan on a guaranteed issue basis, she would likely face a one year exclusion period for pre-existing conditions because the British Healthcare System was not considered creditable coverage and because she was not a HIPAA-eligible person. Fortunately, Martin and Debby moved to Massachusetts during an Open Enrollment Period and the whole family was able to be covered. Although the family was told by Connector staff that Debby's claims could be excluded due to a pre-existing condition exclusion, Debby's claims were not denied.

Moving can lead to a very significant coverage trap. Many Plans like Health Maintenance Organizations (HMOs) and Medicare Advantage Plans are tied to a specific geographic area by law. You must live in that area to be eligible for the coverage. Outside of the area, benefits are limited to urgent and emergent care. Know the specifics of your Plan.

Individual insurance in the private marketplace is regulated by states and, as we have seen, state environments vary. Even if you have the type of insurance product that allows you access to a national network, that doesn't mean you can choose to live anywhere you want and keep that Plan. Make sure.

With insurance coverage you don't ever want to allow yourself or someone you love to be at risk because the insurer decides that you or a family member is not eligible for the coverage. Even with Medicare products which will be discussed later in this book, state of residence matters. Medicare Advantage Plans are always tied to a geographic area, as are Medicare Part D Plans and Medicare Supplements. Your coverage should align with your permanent state of residence.

COMPANY ACQUISITION

Many small companies don't offer benefits or only subsidize them for the employee, not dependents. As a result, when your small company is acquired by a larger company with good group coverage and if you keep your job in that transition, you are typically far better off unless you already had good coverage through your spouse's Plan.

When companies of comparable size merge it is still very important to understand the differences in the Plans and how they might affect you and your family. Domestic partner issues can be particularly troublesome.

Domestic Partner with AIDS Denied Coverage when Company Acquired

Harry had been covered for years as a domestic partner under Matt's large group policy. Harry was dying from AIDS when Matt's company was acquired. Matt was informed that the new company didn't recognize domestic partners as being eligible for coverage but Harry would be able to elect COBRA. This was devastating news since Harry was gravely ill. Matt was first told Harry could have

COBRA for 18 months but at our suggestion challenged that and the COBRA coverage period was increased to 36 months. The cost of the premium was an added burden during this time but at least Harry had coverage. Harry died during the COBRA period.

Selling Business
and Staying on Buyer's Plan

Maureen was 68 when she sold her business. She negotiated staying on the Group Plan for two years after the sale. When that period ended, Social Security told her she had missed her Medicare Part B Special Enrollment Period. She could apply for Part B during the next General Enrollment Period but she would have a gap in coverage and pay lifetime penalties. She went back to the buyers of her business who agreed to let her remain on the Group Plan to avoid a gap in coverage until her Medicare Part B was in place. Was Maureen truly eligible to be on that Plan? Maybe not but large, self-insured employers have more latitude in this regard than others.

Company Acquisition Reduces Union
and Retiree Benefits

Sometimes a cost-cutting strategy when a company is acquired is to reduce expensive healthcare benefits.

Daniel had been the Chairman and CEO of a large U.S. company that had fallen on hard times as it struggled to compete in a more global economy. He had retired with medical benefits through the company and had enrolled in Medicare Part A and B when he turned 65. When Daniel's former company ultimately declared bankruptcy and restructured, it was the perfect opportunity for the union Plan's rich benefits to be reduced and the retiree Plan eliminated altogether. When Daniel received notice of the termination of his retiree medical, he and his wife enrolled in a Medicare Supplement and a Medicare Prescription Drug Plan at their own expense. When Daniel was CEO, he assumed that he and his wife would have generous, subsidized, lifetime retiree medical benefits. It wasn't meant to be. Retiree medical benefits for professionals are particularly vulnerable to being reduced or eliminated because the benefits are usually provided at the company's discretion.

ADULT DISABLED CHILDREN

Some companies allow adult disabled children to remain on a parent's Plan long after a healthier dependent would "age-off." This can be an enormously important protection particularly if the disabled person is in a state where insurance is medically underwritten. How the government handles Social Security Disability Income (SSDI) and Social Security Income (SSI) for these individuals and how they qualify for Medicaid and/or Medicare is beyond the scope of this book. However, in addition to any government benefits to which an adult disabled child may be entitled, anyone who has a disabled adult child should know whether that individual can be covered on a parent's group Health Plan.

Similarly, if you already have an adult disabled child on your Plan know that the coverage will probably terminate as soon as the parent retires. Also, in the case of many adults with chronic mental illness, substance abuse problems, or other issues from which they can recover, the adult disabled child's condition can improve to the point where they no longer meet the criteria to remain on the Plan. Obviously this is joyous news on the one hand but losing good group coverage is never joyous news. At that point, other options have to be anticipated and planned for.

Adult disabled children who may be able to stay on a parent's Plan often become ineligible once the parent retires.

Adult Son with Limited Policy
Diagnosed with Serious Illness

Jeff and Mary had a 28 year old son, Kevin, who had his own limited individual Plan since he had no benefits at work. He had been a totally healthy young man so a cheap Plan with limited benefits seemed to make sense at the time. Subsequently, Kevin was diagnosed with a very aggressive type of leukemia. Mary contacted her Benefits Department about getting Kevin on her Plan. Kevin was so incapacitated that he met the criteria for an adult disabled child but Mary had just missed the open enrollment deadline for adding him to her coverage. We urged her to plead for an exception that would result in Kevin's enrollment on the Plan. The Benefits Department didn't believe they had the authority to make an exception for Kevin. The matter was discussed with the President of the company who approved allowing Kevin to come on the Plan. The open enrollment deadline had passed but the company made an exception since the coverage year had not yet begun.

The lesson here is that although one can't expect special consideration, it never hurts to ask for it.

Adult Child
Health Status Improves

Bill's son, Rob, had a history of substance abuse issues that were serious enough to have him deemed disabled and eligible to be on his father's Plan. Each year the Plan requested physician notes to assess Rob's ability to remain on the Plan. Happily Rob had turned his life around. He was able to maintain a steady job although at a low rate of pay at a local store which offered no benefits. But he was living alone and maintained sobriety. After reviewing the most recent physician notes requested, the Plan indicated that Rob did not meet the criteria for remaining on his father's group Plan as a disabled adult.

Rob was eligible for three years of COBRA and lived in a state with a High Risk Pool. Worst case, he could use his federal COBRA and HIPAA protections to maintain coverage since he'd likely be denied coverage in the individual marketplace because a health questionnaire would ask about his substance abuse history and he would be deemed a poor risk. Fortunately, Rob's family could afford to pay for the coverage he needed.

Plan rules allowing adult disabled children to remain on family insurance vary. Verify what your adult disabled child's rights are.

Group Coverage Traps and Gaps

Many individuals are rather cavalier about any perils associated with coverage as a result of changing jobs because they've successfully navigated this transition numerous times in the past without any negative consequences. In my view that is often because the family is in good health not because the coverage is similar. The system works to the extent it does because most of us have reasonably good group benefits and are healthy.

Mr. and Mrs. Stevens, one of the case examples from the beginning of the book, were innocent victims of the gift of inferior coverage as a result of a promotion within the same company which involved a move to another state. Their identification cards were inexplicably delayed and the cards were misleading. A logo on them suggested out-of-network benefits when there were none. The materials describing their Plan followed months after the identification cards and were also misleading. It turned out they had been enrolled in a closed panel HMO with no out-of-network benefits. This wouldn't have mattered to them had Mrs. Stevens not been diagnosed with breast cancer.

As mentioned before, the traps associated with group coverage or changing group coverage are often not as dramatic as those associated with losing group coverage but they are real. Some of the unfortunate situations we've encountered when our client is starting a new position, working a reduced work schedule, having a group Plan that imposes pre-existing condition exclusions, or selecting among open enrollment options are discussed in this chapter.

WAITING PERIODS

You may have no control over what happens to your group benefits. You have a job and the benefits change or you accept a new job and the coverage options are what they are. **However, one issue individuals can control in a transition is making sure they don't have a gap of 63 days or more when moving from one job with good group benefits to another job with good group benefits.** If you have a gap of more than 63 days, you leave yourself vulnerable to a pre-existing condition exclusion which is usually 12 months. That means that no claims will be paid for services associated with a former illness or injury during the exclusion period.

As discussed under the HIPAA section of the book, comprehensive coverage without a gap in coverage of more than 63 days prevents the new Plan from imposing pre-existing condition exclusions. That coverage must be "creditable." In some situations, a new Plan can impose a pre-existing condition exclusion period if your former coverage didn't include the same class of benefits. For example, if you move from insurance that has no out-of-network benefits to coverage that has out-of-network benefits, the new insurer may be able to exclude coverage under the out-of-network benefits for a period of time. This is not always true but it is a possibility you should be aware of.

NEW JOB TRAPS

It is not unusual to find yourself ensnared in going from one job with benefits to another job with benefits and assuming coverage is more similar than it is. It's always wise to review coverage that may be offered to you at as detailed a level as possible.

In my experience, parents of special needs children are among the most "healthcare coverage savvy" Americans. But even an extremely informed consumer, a father of a special needs child, can fall into a trap as did our client on the next page.

> *When starting a new job, plan for no gap in coverage. If there is a gap, make sure it is not 63 days or longer. If that happens, the new Plan may impose a pre-existing condition exclusion period.*

New Job with Promise of Good Benefits for Autistic Child

Patrick was considering a good offer from another company. They wanted him and he wanted the job. The only problem: the youngest of Patrick's three children was autistic. Sam, the autistic child, was doing reasonably well but he still needed a great deal of physical therapy and speech therapy to make sure he didn't regress. Patrick met personally with the head of Human Resources at the new firm. She explained that their company's richest Plan provided for up to 90 visits of physical and speech therapy and reassured him that Sam would be entitled to those services. Having validated that this was even better coverage than the family now had, Patrick took the job.

A few months later all of Sam's physical and speech therapy claims had been denied. Patrick called the insurer and learned that the physical and speech therapy benefits were limited to those with "injury or illness." In fact, there was a specific exclusion for services provided for congenital conditions. Patrick was devastated. He met with the Human Resources executive who had assured him services would be covered. She hadn't read the fine print in the Evidence of Coverage document and was also devastated. Patrick learned the hard way that he had taken a position with a self-insured company that had great latitude to decide what benefits to offer under federal law at that time. Because the company was not regulated by the State Insurance Department, the company had no obligation to provide even the minimum therapy benefits required by state law.

The Human Resources Executive said she would discuss the matter with the CEO to see if they could provide some special assistance to Patrick's family while they investigated the potential issues associated with changing the benefit. Patrick thought through everything to assure coverage for his son's services before taking the new job. "I couldn't have done anything differently," he said. "When the head of Human Resources doesn't even know what's covered, what chance does anyone have?"

Pre-Existing Condition Issues:
Full- to Part-Time

A reduced work schedule can trigger a loss in your coverage and benefits as discussed below.

> Mr. Jones had worked for the local hospital for decades. In an effort to cut expenses the hospital was offering a number of employees the opportunity to work a reduced schedule over the summer. Mr. Jones was assured he could return to full time duties in the fall. Anyway, he liked the idea of having more time off during the summer. The only problem was that the summer schedule would trigger a loss in coverage because he wouldn't be working enough hours to qualify for the group Plan. He was told he'd get a COBRA notice and could elect COBRA.
>
> Mr. Jones got the COBRA notice and was shocked at how expensive COBRA was. He decided to go without insurance for the three months. After all, he and his wife had been covered their whole lives and had hardly used it. He didn't think that three months without coverage would be a problem. Toward the end of the three month period, Mrs. Jones who had always had coverage through her husband's Plan, was advised she needed surgery. Until this happened she did not know that Mr. Jones had let the coverage lapse. She called our office and we advised her that the safest course was to see if they could elect COBRA retroactively so they had no gap in coverage. The union said no. The COBRA deadline had passed. However, union officials assured Mr. and Mrs. Jones she could have the surgery after Mr. Jones resumed his full time work schedule and no pre-existing condition exclusions would be imposed.

Our experience with denied claims as a result of a pre-existing condition exclusion, made us nervous about relying on assurance from the union. Nevertheless claims were paid. Mr. and Mrs. Jones were very, very lucky that this union coverage came through even though their coverage gap went beyond the 63 day rule. Luck is good but you can't always rely on luck in today's environment. Contrast the Jones experience with an attempted denial of a surgery claim for my son who has had continuous group coverage his entire life.

Pre-existing Condition Issues: Group Coverage

At times when I have counseled clients to avoid a gap in coverage of 63 days, they're rather skeptical that this can be a problem. As a result, I have been asked if insurers actually impose pre-existing condition exclusions. The answer is "yes." Let me tell you my son's story:

> Paul was a college student scheduled for day surgery during Christmas break in December 2004. The procedure was scheduled with an in-network surgeon and was pre-authorized. It had already been determined that the procedure was medically necessary. Nevertheless, the surgeon's claim was denied due to a pre-existing condition. The Plan wasn't going to pay the surgeon. The explanation of benefit form indicated we had no responsibility to pay him either. I felt badly for this in-network surgeon because the procedure had been pre-authorized. I was annoyed.
>
> I called the service center and told the representative that to deny the claim due to a pre-existing condition was a violation of federal HIPAA laws. After conferring with his supervisor, he agreed that I was correct but that in order to consider reprocessing the claim they would need a certificate of creditable coverage showing Paul's continuous group coverage. I told him my son who was 21 at the time had had continuous coverage his entire life and only had to show continuous coverage for 18 months to prevent a pre-existing condition exclusion. I went on to say that I wasn't sure how long we had had United Healthcare but at least four years and if he could agree that four years was longer than 18 months (which by the way he could check in his system), they had to process the claim. He spoke to his supervisor again and reported to me that the claim was being forwarded to "the rapid resolution unit."

UNITED HEALTHCARE SERVICE LLC
TAMPA SERVICE CENTER
P O BOX 740800
ATLANTA, GA 30374-0800
PHONE: (800) 638-5199
VISIT WWW.MYUHC.COM FOR SELF-SERVICE

UnitedHealthcare
A UnitedHealth Group Company

PAGE: 1 OF 1
DATE: 02/21/05
ID #: E 000095868
EMPLOYEE: JOHN CARLEY
CONTRACT: 0185807
BENEFIT PLAN: CONSOLIDATED EDISON OF NY

JOHN CARLEY

DARIEN CT

EXPLANATION
OF BENEFITS

SERVICE DETAIL

PATIENT/RELAT CLAIM NUMBER	PROVIDER/ SERVICE	DATE OF SERVICE	AMOUNT CHARGED	NOT COVERED	AMOUNT ALLOWED	COPAY/ DEDUCTIBLE	PLAN COVERS	BENEFIT AVAILABLE	REMARK CODE
PAUL ST H 4173446101	SURGERY	12/21/04	3100.00					0.00*	CM
	SURGERY	12/21/04	3100.00					0.00*	CM
	TOTAL		6200.00					0.00	K9

PLAN PAYS	0.00	
** PATIENT PAYS	0.00	

(*) INDICATES PAYMENT ASSIGNED TO PROVIDER

** DEFINITION: "PATIENT PAYS" IS THE AMOUNT, IF ANY, OWED YOUR PROVIDER. THIS MAY INCLUDE AMOUNTS ALREADY PAID TO YOUR PROVIDER AT TIME OF SERVICE.

REMARK CODE(S) LISTED BELOW ARE REFERENCED IN THE "SERVICE DETAIL" SECTION UNDER THE HEADING "REMARK CODE"
(CM) YOUR GROUP HEALTH PLAN CONTAINS A PRE-EXISTING CONDITION LIMITATION. SINCE THESE EXPENSES RELATE TO A CONDITION WHICH WE HAVE DETERMINED FALL UNDER THE PRE-EXISTING LIMITATION, NO COMPREHENSIVE OR MAJOR MEDICAL BENEFITS ARE AVAILABLE AT THIS TIME.
(K9) THIS IS A RECONSIDERATION OF CHARGES PREVIOUSLY PROCESSED. YOUR ENROLLMENT AND ELIGIBILITY QUESTIONS WERE RESOLVED.

BENEFIT PLAN PAYMENT SUMMARY INFORMATION

$0.00

SATISFIED 2004 TO-DATE	OUT OF POCKET	OUT OF NETWORK DEDUCTIBLE	LIFETIME MAXIMUM REMAINING
PAUL ST	$0.00	$0.00	$1986070.79
PLAN YEAR 2004	INDIV: $1400.00	INDIV: $350.00	LIFETIME PLAN MAXIMUM $2000000.00

A REVIEW OF THIS BENEFIT DETERMINATION MAY BE REQUESTED BY SUBMITTING YOUR APPEAL TO US IN WRITING AT THE FOLLOWING ADDRESS: UNITEDHEALTHCARE APPEALS, P.O. BOX 30432, SALT LAKE CITY, UT 84130-0432. THE REQUEST FOR YOUR REVIEW MUST BE MADE WITHIN 180 DAYS FROM THE DATE YOU RECEIVE THIS STATEMENT. IF YOU REQUEST A REVIEW OF YOUR CLAIM DENIAL, WE WILL COMPLETE OUR REVIEW NOT LATER THAN 30 DAYS AFTER WE RECEIVE YOUR REQUEST FOR REVIEW.

YOU MAY HAVE THE RIGHT TO FILE A CIVIL ACTION UNDER ERISA IF ALL REQUIRED REVIEWS OF YOUR CLAIM HAVE BEEN COMPLETED.

* * * * * * *

YOU CAN MEET MANY OF YOUR NEEDS ONLINE AT WWW.MYUHC.COM. AT ALMOST ANYTIME DAY OR NIGHT, YOU CAN REVIEW CLAIMS, CHECK ELIGIBILITY, LOCATE A NETWORK PHYSICIAN, REQUEST AN ID CARD, REFILL PRESCRIPTIONS IF ELIGIBLE, AND MORE! FOR IMMEDIATE, SECURE SELF-SERVICE, VISIT WWW.MYUHC.COM.

HOW TO REGISTER?
YOU CAN REGISTER AND BEGIN USING MYUHC IN THE SAME SESSION. ACCESS WWW.MYUHC.COM TO REGISTER. THE INFORMATION REQUIRED IS ON YOUR INSURANCE ID CARD (FIRST NAME, LAST NAME, MEMBER ID, GROUP NUMBER AND DATE OF BIRTH).

* * * * * * *

MAINTAINING THE PRIVACY AND SECURITY OF INDIVIDUALS' PERSONAL INFORMATION IS VERY IMPORTANT TO US AT UNITEDHEALTHCARE. TO PROTECT YOUR PRIVACY, WE HAVE IMPLEMENTED STRICT CONFIDENTIALITY PRACTICES. THESE PRACTICES INCLUDE THE ABILITY TO USE A UNIQUE INDIVIDUAL IDENTIFIER. YOU MAY SEE THE UNIQUE INDIVIDUAL IDENTIFIER ON UNITEDHEALTHCARE CORRESPONDENCE, INCLUDING MEDICAL ID CARDS (IF APPLICABLE), LETTERS, EXPLANATION OF BENEFITS (EOBS) AND PROVIDER REMITTANCE ADVICES (PRAS). IF YOU HAVE ANY QUESTIONS ABOUT THE UNIQUE INDIVIDUAL IDENTIFIER OR ITS USE, PLEASE CONTACT YOUR CUSTOMER CARE PROFESSIONAL AT THE NUMBER SHOWN AT THE TOP OF THIS STATEMENT.

THIS IS NOT A BILL

United Healthcare explanation of benefits
statement—claim denied due to pre-existing
condition exclusion, a violation of federal
HIPAA law due to no gap in coverage.

Why would United Healthcare have denied this claim based on a pre-existing condition when they had no right to deny for that reason? Unfortunately, I can't know the answer. The denial delayed payment to the doctor for several months leaving an in-network physician in a vulnerable position. He operated in good faith, relying on the pre-authorization only to have the surgery claim retroactively denied. We'll never know if the doctor's staff would have resolved the situation and received payment without my intervention. Remember, as long as you have had continuous creditable coverage for 18 months or longer with no gap in coverage of 63 days or more, an insurer cannot deny a claim because of a pre-existing condition exclusion.

> *If you've had creditable coverage for 18 months or longer, a group health Plan cannot deny a medically necessary claim based on a pre-existing condition.*

OPEN ENROLLMENT

Open Enrollment is that one time of year during which larger employers allow employees who are fortunate enough to have coverage choices, to move from one Plan to another. The trend is often in a direction of fewer choices or no choices or more complexity but every so often we stumble across an employer still providing a dizzying array of Plan choices.

Evaluating options involves weighing how comprehensive the coverage is, its potential cost to you, the provider network and the hassle factor, meaning does the Plan require a referral to see a specialist or is it an "open-access" Plan not requiring a referral, what are the pre-authorization requirements and penalties, etc. Don't be fooled. At times a higher cost option is not the best option. There isn't necessarily a "right" answer. A decision should be based on your personal circumstances, priorities and values with the hope that you don't have remorse over the decision you made later in the year.

Selecting a Plan from Numerous Options

Carolyn and her family had sole proprietor coverage through her freelance work. She loved the work, freedom and flexibility but when a large non-profit organization offered her a full time position with everything she'd dreamed of she couldn't resist. Soon after starting the job Carolyn learned she'd been diagnosed with an aggressive cancer. Making the correct choice among her six Plan options had never been so important. Carolyn was leaning toward the indemnity Plan but contacted us to help her make a decision.

The indemnity Plan looked attractive on paper because Carolyn could go to any provider but it wasn't structured with an in-network benefit and an out-of-pocket maximum, so Carolyn could have ended up like Joanne Yamamoto, with unlimited out-of-pocket expenses after insurance paid.

We reviewed Carolyn's options. Carolyn expected to receive all services through doctors affiliated with a single medical center. We recommended a Plan where all her doctors and other providers would be in-network with no referral requirement. Carolyn had good financial protection from unexpected medical bills after insurance paid. A little more than a year later, Carolyn died. Her premature death is tragic but at least she didn't leave her family with medical bills that might have taken years to pay.

EVALUATING GROUP COVERAGE OPTIONS

Whenever you're in a fortunate enough position to have choice among many different coverage options, carefully analyze the situation. Home in on in-network out-of-pocket maximums. Out-of-network out-of-pocket maximums can be misleading because when you see an out-of-network provider there is no contract between your Plan and the provider. As a result, the excess charges beyond what the insurer deemed reasonable and customary is not applied to an out-of-pocket maximum. If financial protection is important to you, then you must focus on the provider network and the in-network out-of-pocket maximum to minimize your financial exposure.

Background Information

T his section of the book provides important information about Medicare and Medicare-related products. Medicare has become increasingly complex and now that Medicare Part B and Part D premiums are income-indexed, you want to pay what you should for Medicare and related products but not overpay.

For more information, call 1-800-MEDICARE or 1-800-633-4227. Important information is also on-line at www.medicare.gov.

MEDICARE PREMIUM PENALTIES

One of the primary objectives of this book is to educate those who work beyond age 65 about the importance of handling their Special Enrollment onto Medicare properly in order to avoid premium penalties. Premium penalties exist so that people who missed their Initial Enrollment Period or their Special Enrollment Period (if entitled to one) will pay more when they enroll. This is to discourage people from waiting until they're sick to enroll in Medicare.

Some people working beyond age 65 can postpone getting onto Medicare, particularly Part B, because they can choose to remain on group coverage. This is true of people who work for companies of 20 or more people or who are married to someone working at a company of 20 or more people and maintain coverage through those companies. We have seen many people rather innocently run afoul of Special Enrollment rules for Medicare Part B for the various reasons I'll describe. Part B premium penalties are **life-time** premium penalties. Read about Mr. Moore in the Special Enrollment

Examples. He sold his business at 78 and took COBRA. He missed his Special Enrollment and paid Part B penalties assessed back 14 years (to age 65, his Initial Enrollment Period) for life and had no medical coverage immediately following surgery.

Medicare Part D recognizes creditable coverage with the 63 day HIPAA-eligible transition timeframe. Part B has unique rules so please read about Part B Special Enrollment carefully.

Part A penalties are only assessed to people who didn't earn "premium-free" Part A so have to pay a premium for their Part A and didn't start paying as soon as they were eligible to "buy-in." Few people pay Part A penalties. Part B and D penalties are another matter. Because our taxes pay for so much of Part B and D, as a matter of policy, the government wants everyone paying in as soon as possible.

> *Medicare Part B premium penalties associated with missing a Special Enrollment Period are **lifetime** premium penalties.*

EXHAUSTING MEDICARE PART A HOSPITALIZATION COVERAGE

It is vitally important to understand how Medicare Part A hospital and skilled nursing benefits work and how they can be exhausted. This is not a common problem but can be so financially devastating that it should be understood. In 2001, I saw for the first time a Medicare Summary Notice (MSN) showing that Part A had been exhausted. The MSN stated," You may be billed $386,639.16" and sure enough the patient's estate was billed that amount by the Hospital. You should know about this risk and how to protect your family from it. The gentleman who died had what he thought was comprehensive retiree coverage through an affluent Fairfield County, Connecticut town but the retiree medical benefits did not include catastrophic hospitalization coverage which is addressed on page 149.

A more recent experience with a client in this situation resulted in an $800,939.00 hospital bill. Charges were $6,156.00 per day. Medicare Part A benefits were exhausted and our client's secondary coverage lifetime maximum was exhausted. ACA requires the former employer to assume more risk for these types of bills. As a result, I believe we should expect more changes to retiree benefits for those 65 and over.

MEDICARE BEFORE AGE 65

Some people are eligible for Medicare before 65. In 1972 Medicare benefits were extended to people who have end stage renal disease and also to those who are deemed totally disabled. In 2000, Medicare benefits were extended to those who have been diagnosed with ALS or Lou Gehrig's disease. This book addresses the issues common to most of us who qualify for Medicare at 65.

WHO NEEDS THIS INFORMATION?

Everyone on Medicare or planning to go on Medicare will benefit from the information in this book. We have assisted clients for years with transitions to Medicare. We have also dealt with clients who didn't get good advice at the front end and came to us in crisis or dispute. Many of these situations were entirely avoidable; many of them were heartbreaking.

HISTORY OF MEDICARE

Medicare provides hospital (Part A), medical (Part B) and drug coverage (Part D) to most retired Americans age 65 and over. The legislation creating Medicare was passed in 1965 and the program began in 1966. Medicare was structured like the major medical Plans that existed in the 1960s, largely intended to cover illnesses or injuries rather than well-care, but over the years coverage for many preventive services has been added.

Medicare does not cover services provided outside the United States except in situations where someone becomes ill close to the Mexican or Canadian borders or in Canada en route to Alaska. You obtain coverage for services outside the United States by using travel insurance, a Medicare Supplement, a Medicare Advantage Plan, or your retiree medical coverage.

Many more changes to Medicare are part of ACA, the reform legislation of 2010, but given the uncertainty surrounding that law, it's impossible to predict what may happen.

MEDICARE · MEDICAID
Health Care Financing Administration

Medicare Summary Notice

CUSTOMER SERVICE INFORMATION

Your Medicare Number:

If you have questions, write or call:
Empire Medicare Services
Beneficiary Inquiries
P.O. Box 4846
Syracuse, NY 13221-4846

Toll-free:	**1-800-442-8430**
Spanish:	1-800-492-6879
TTY for Hearing Impaired:	1-877-623-6190

HELP STOP FRAUD: Be informed - Read your Medicare Summary Notice.

This is a summary of claims processed on 09/14/2001.

PART A HOSPITAL INSURANCE - INPATIENT CLAIMS

Dates of Service	Benefit Days Used	Non-Covered Charges	Deductible and Coinsurance	You May Be Billed	See Notes Section
Control number					a,b,c
Referred by: 06/02/00-07/26/01	150 days	$356,763.16	$29,876.00	$386,639.16	d,e,f, g

Notes Section:

a This is a correction to a previously processed claim and/or deductible record.

b 60 of the Benefit Days Used were charged to your Lifetime Reserve Day benefit.

c These services cannot be paid because your benefits are exhausted at this time.

(continued)

THIS IS NOT A BILL - Keep this notice for your records.

Medicare summary notice showing Medicare
hospital benefit exhausted.

MEDICARE HAS BECOME MORE EXPENSIVE

Although employers and workers pay for Medicare Part A, Medicare Parts B and D are heavily subsidized by taxpayers. In fact, 75% of the cost of Part B is paid for through general tax revenues or our income tax dollars. For the first 40 years of the Medicare program, everyone paid the same Part B premiums. But in 2007, Part B premiums became income-indexed.

RECENT HISTORY OF MONTHLY PART B PREMIUMS—PER PERSON

Year	Premium/Premium Range (Higher Premiums Based on Income)
2000	$45.50
2006	$88.50
2007*	$93.50–$254.90
2011*	$96.40–$369.10
2012*	$99.90–$319.70

Higher premiums are paid by individuals with incomes greater than $85,000.00 and couples with incomes over $170,000.00.

There are times when those on Social Security pay lower Part B premiums than individuals who are not yet taking Social Security retirement benefits. When there is no cost-of-living adjustment to Social Security retirement benefits, Part B premiums do not increase. In addition to Part B premiums being income-indexed, Part D premiums became income-indexed in 2011. The ACA calls for Medicare payroll taxes to be increased substantially in 2013. In addition, new taxes on unearned income will also be implemented in 2013 to help pay for Medicare Part A.

> *Until 2007, everyone's Part B premium penalties were heavily subsidized by taxpayers. The current system charges any individual with income of $85,000+ an income-indexed premium.*

CHANGING DEMOGRAPHICS

Medicare worked well for many years largely because of fundamental demographics. The proportion of the population on Medicare was small relative to the proportion of workers paying into the system and/or paying taxes to support Medicare. Now that equation is reversing as the "baby-boomers" age onto Medicare.

As we regularly read in the newspapers, Medicare is under great financial strain. The surprising reduction in 2012 versus 2011 Part B premiums is welcome but far from a trend. Particularly disturbing is the increasing number of doctors, especially primary care doctors, who are limiting the number of Medicare patients in their practices, not taking new Medicare patients at all, maintaining a waiting list or opting out of Medicare altogether.

WHO DOESN'T GET MEDICARE?

If you didn't work the required years in a job that pays into Social Security or weren't married to someone long enough who did pay in, you don't qualify for premium-free Medicare Part A. Over the years, I have dealt with many people who thought all Americans are eligible for Medicare regardless of their work record. This is not true.

MEDICARE IS COMPLEX AND HAS BECOME MORE COMPLEX

Let's spend a moment on the "alphabet soup" of Medicare. When Medicare was enacted, there was just Medicare Part A and B. Later, private Supplements, so-called Medi-gap Plans, A through J, were added. These are private insurance products that provide additional coverage. The private Supplements are not a government benefit. After that, Medicare Part C (now Advantage Plans) were implemented in 1997. Medicare Advantage Plans are private Plans one can choose as an alternative to original Medicare. Most recently, Medicare Part D became effective in 2006.

At times we hear that Medicare is simple, even cheap, to administer. Medicare claims are relatively straightforward to administer but administration of the Medicare program has become more complicated. In addition to the Centers for Medicare and Medicaid Services, the Social Security Administration is involved because Social Security manages most Medicare enrollment. The Railroad Retirement Board (RRB) handles enrollment for railroad retirees. Social Security and RRB also pay Medicare Prescription Drug Plan and Medicare Advantage Plan premiums on behalf of beneficiaries who've elected such deductions. The Internal Revenue Service is involved, too. The IRS provides tax information to Social Security and the RRB every year which is used to determine income-adjusted Part B and D premiums for higher income Americans.

We have dealt with many people over the years who didn't know if they had enrolled in Medicare Part A and/or B usually because they still had large group coverage through an employer which was primary at the time. You should always know and understand what's on your Medicare card. The card will have your Part A (Hospital) Insurance effective date and Part B (Medical) insurance effective date.

Unless you are eligible for Railroad Retirement benefits, your Medicare card has a suffix and there are numerous suffixes, 204 at last count. Suffixes provide information to Social Security about your status. If you paid into Social Security yourself and are getting Social Security benefits, your Medicare number will be your Social Security number with an "A" as a suffix. If you paid into Social Security on your work record but are not yet receiving Social Security retirement benefits, your Medicare number will be your Social Security number with a "T" on the end. This will change to an "A" once you start getting Social Security.

It gets worse. Let's say you were an at-home Mom whose spouse paid into Social Security. In that situation, you are eligible for Medicare based on your spouse's work record. Until your spouse starts collecting Social Security, your Medicare number will be your Social Security number with an "A" suffix. Later it will change to your spouse's Social Security number, generally with a "B" suffix. If your spouse predeceases you, you'll get a new card with a "D" suffix and if you were divorced to a spouse who paid in, your suffix will be a "D" sometimes followed by a number. Very simple indeed.

> *Different federal agencies administer portions of the Medicare program. You enroll in Medicare Parts A and B through Social Security or the Railroad Retirement Board, not through Medicare.*

These As, Bs and Ds after your Medicare number on your Medicare card have nothing whatsoever to do with Medicare Parts A, B or D. They also have nothing to do with private Medicare Supplements A, B or D. Your Medicare card only provides information about Medicare Parts A and B. **Your Medicare card will never indicate your Part D enrollment, Supplement Enrollment or whether you are in a Medicare Advantage Plan.**

I'm not making Medicare confusing. Until you're familiar with these issues, Medicare *is* confusing.

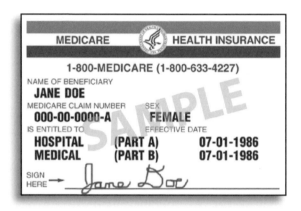

RECENT MEDICARE CHANGES INCLUDE:

* **2006:** Medicare Part D for outpatient drug coverage is implemented. Part D is a government benefit administered by private companies. Unlike Medicare Part A or Medicare Part B, you also have to select a Plan for Part D.
* **2007:** Medicare Part B, which covers outpatient services, became income-indexed.
* **2010:** More changes occur in the private Supplement market. Plans E, H, I and J were eliminated; M and N were added.
* **2011:** Part D premiums became income-indexed. The ACA provided a 50% discount on brand name drugs for those in the "donut" hole or gap.

Medicare Parts A and B and Enrollment Traps

The following section briefly defines what Medicare Parts A and B cover and describes the various sources of payment among employers, taxpayers and individuals. Medicare Parts A and B are original Medicare, the core of the Medicare Program. A discussion of Medicare Enrollment issues also follows. Understanding Medicare's enrollment rules is critically important for anyone planning a transition onto Medicare.

What does Medicare Part A (hospital insurance) cover?

Most inpatient services (with some exceptions) as follows:

+ An inpatient hospital admission of three days or more
+ A medically necessary (meeting Medicare criteria) skilled nursing or rehabilitation facility admission following or within 30 days of a hospital admission for the same reason
+ Home health services associated with and following the inpatient hospital and/or skilled facility
+ Hospice services—often provided in the home to those who are terminally ill at the end of life

Who pays for Medicare Part A?

Medicare Part A is paid by active employees and their employers. The 2.9% Medicare tax on payroll is split between the employee and employer, 1.45% each. This amount is taken out of every paycheck.

You typically qualify for Medicare Part A because you worked for (roughly) ten years or had a long enough marriage to someone who paid into Social Security for ten years. Americans who don't qualify and "buy-in" to Medicare Part A will pay $451.00 per month in 2012.

The ACA calls for significant tax increases in 2013 to help fund Medicare Part A: an additional .9% payroll tax contribution from higher income workers, maxing out at 2.35% total, and taxes on unearned income. The taxes apply to individuals earning $200,000.00 or couples earning $250,000.00. A new 3.8% tax on investment income will apply to income from interest, dividends, annuities, royalties, rent and capital gains. Medicare has never historically taxed unearned income. Thus, as of 2013, affluent retirees will continue to pay for Part A for their entire lives in addition to active employees/employers (at least as long as they remain affluent).

What does Medicare Part B (medical insurance) cover?

Most physician and outpatient services (the following is not a complete listing):

- Physician services, including surgery
- Chemotherapy
- Outpatient hospital procedures (at hospitals and other facilities)
- Physical therapy and other outpatient rehabilitation services
- Lab, and durable medical equipment like crutches or wheelchairs

Who pays for Medicare Part B?

Taxpayers pay roughly 75% of what Part B costs and those enrolled in Part B pay the balance. Those paying the highest Part B premiums in 2012, $319.70 per month, are paying about 80% of their Part B as opposed to most Americans who pay the standard premium or about 25% of the government's projected cost of Part B. No one pays more than 80% of the projected cost of Part B regardless of your income.

When should I enroll in Medicare A and B?

For anyone about to turn 65, this is the most important section of this book. Always remember that Medicare's enrollment rules are strict and unforgiving and designed to penalize anyone who doesn't follow them, sometimes with **lifetime** premium penalties and a gap in coverage. A chart summarizing helpful information about enrolling in Medicare is shown on the following page.

TRANSITION TO MEDICARE CONSIDERATIONS

(Simplified for illustration purposes)

SITUATION	MEDICARE A	MEDICARE B	PART D AND SUPPLEMENT OR ADVANTAGE PLAN (WITH PART D)	RETIREE
Receiving Social Security. At 64 and nine months	Auto-enrolled by Social Security.	Auto-enrolled by Social Security. (May opt out if active group through spouse, business more than 20 employees).	Consider Part D Plan and private Supplement or Advantage Plan unless active group coverage or retiree coverage in effect.	If eligible, company will require you to be enrolled in Medicare A and B. You rarely need D.
Not receiving Social Security. At 64 and nine months	Enroll through Social Security (unless active Health Savings Account Plan).	Enroll through Social Security (unless active group through work or spouse's work in business more than 20 employees.)	Consider Part D Plan and private Supplement or Advantage Plan unless active group coverage or retiree coverage in effect.	If eligible, company will require you to be enrolled in Medicare A and B. You rarely need D.
Have active group coverage through work or spouse's work. Business has 20 or more employees.	Enroll through Social Security (unless choose to remain active in Health Savings Account).	Part B optional in this scenario. Weigh pros and cons.	Don't consider these options until retirement or spouse's retirement.	Not applicable.
Have active group coverage through work or spouse's work. Business fewer than 20 employees.	Enroll through Social Security (unless active Health Savings Account Plan).	Enroll through Social Security (most Plans require Part B enrollment).	Don't consider these options until retirement or spouse's retirement.	Not applicable.
Retiring or spouse retiring after age 65.	Enroll through Social Security (if not already enrolled).	Enroll within eight months of active work and usually to coincide with retirement.	Consider Part D and Supplement or Advantage Plan unless transitioning onto retiree medical with drug coverage.	If eligible, company will require you to be enrolled in Medicare A and B. You rarely need D.
Medicare Part A: Hospital Insurance	*Medicare Part B: Medical Insurance*	*Medicare Part D: Prescription Drug Coverage*	*Medicare Advantage: Alternative to original Medicare A and B. May or may not include Drug.*	*Retiree Medical: Through former employer, secondary to Medicare. Usually includes Drug.*

If you are already getting Social Security prior to age 65, Social Security will enroll you in Medicare Parts A and B and automatically send you a card. In that case, should you have active group coverage through a spouse in a group of over 20 employees, you might want to consider opting out of Part B. However, those who are not taking Social Security retirement benefits at age 65 but who need Medicare at age 65 must enroll through Social Security, not Medicare, for Parts A and B.

When am I eligible for Medicare?
If you are eligible for Medicare through your own work history or a spouse's, former spouse's or deceased spouse's work record, you are typically eligible for Medicare on the first day of the month of your 65th birthday. If your birthday is on the first of the month, you are eligible on the first of the prior month. This is true of almost everyone except those who qualified before age 65. Those who don't qualify for premium-free Part A are also eligible to buy-in to Medicare at this time.

There are three Enrollment Periods for Medicare Parts A and B.

+ **The Initial Enrollment Period:** For those who need to be enrolled at age 65;
+ **The Special Enrollment Period:** For those who maintain active group coverage after age 65; and
+ **The General Enrollment Period:** For those who 1) didn't manage an Enrollment Period properly or, 2) did not enroll when they could have enrolled but subsequently changed their minds.

> *There are three enrollment periods for Medicare Parts A and B: Initial (around age 65), Special (after losing active group coverage), and General (first quarter of every year). If you enroll during the General, you will likely pay penalties and have a gap in coverage, unless you're close to your 65th birthday.*

The Initial Enrollment Period begins three months before your 65th birthday, includes the month of your birthday, and extends for the three months after your birthday. If you need Medicare as soon as you are first eligible, enroll two or three months before your birthday. If you wait until the month of your birthday or later, your enrollment will be delayed.

Remember, if you have retiree medical through a former employer, you need to be enrolled in Medicare Parts A and B as soon as you are eligible, typically the first of the month you turn 65.

Also, if you have sole proprietor coverage you need to enroll in Medicare at age 65. Medicare does not consider "group of one" coverage as entitling one to a Special Enrollment Period. Even if you have coverage through an Association, Medicare may still consider this sole proprietor coverage since the coverage is based on the fact that you are essentially self-employed. You might be able to keep this coverage as secondary to Medicare but you still need to be enrolled in Medicare Parts A and B. If you have questions about this, contact Social Security.

Self-employed individuals who have sole proprietor coverage are not entitled to a Special Enrollment Period.

How do I enroll in Medicare during the Initial Enrollment Period?
The following is a step-by-step guide to handling the issues associated with enrolling in Medicare during the Initial Enrollment Period.

1. Determine if you need Medicare to be in place at age 65. This is true of virtually everyone except those working for or married to someone working for larger companies of 20 or more employees for whom their group coverage is primary. You ordinarily have to be enrolled in both Medicare Parts A and B if you have coverage through a company of fewer than 20 people but there are exceptions. If your insurance broker says you don't need Part B, you should get a letter verifying you don't need to be enrolled in Part B from the insurer.

2. If you are already receiving Social Security benefits before your 65th birthday, you will automatically be enrolled in Medicare Parts A and B and your Medicare card will be sent to you. If you have other group coverage that is primary through a working spouse, you should consider whether or not you want Medicare Part B. If you choose to opt out, instructions for doing so are on your Medicare card. **If that group Plan has a health savings account an employer contributes to and/ or you want to continue to contribute to the account, you should opt out of Part A, too, under current federal rules.**

3. If you aren't receiving Social Security benefits, you have to enroll in Medicare yourself through Social Security. If you have paid into Social Security as a worker you can even enroll on-line through www.ssa.gov. Go to that website, press "Enroll in Medicare" and proceed through the process. You should know your status with respect to Social Security because workers who've paid in receive an annual statement from Social Security about three months before their birthday. You can also call your local Social Security office and make a telephone or in-person appointment to enroll or call the national Social Security number, 1-800-772-1213. But remember, do this well in advance of the month of your 65th birthday. Better to act early in the Initial Enrollment Period so that you optimize your chances of having your Medicare card before its effective date and just in case anything goes wrong.

4. If you did not pay into Social Security and will be eligible for Medicare through a spouse who is not yet taking Social Security benefits, or a former spouse or deceased spouse, at least for now you can't use the on-line enrollment tool on ssa.gov. In that case you need to contact Social Security.

5. Depending on the information about you in the Social Security system, you may have to produce a birth certificate or a marriage certificate or proof of citizenship. It can seem unnerving to send in these documents to Social Security. If that's a concern to you, then make an in-person appointment.

6. If you are receiving or going to be eligible for Railroad Retirement Benefits, YOU DO NOT GO THROUGH SOCIAL SECURITY TO ENROLL IN MEDICARE. You must work through the Railroad Retirement Board. The timeframes are the same but your Medicare card will have a prefix rather than a suffix and your claims will be processed differently.

7. Be on the look-out for your Medicare card and follow-up if you don't receive it. If you can register on mymedicare.gov, then you know you've been enrolled. When you get your Medicare card be sure that the Medicare Part A and B effective dates on the front of the card match what you expected.

8. Early in the Initial Enrollment Period you should determine what kind of insurance you want in place in addition to Medicare Parts A and B and manage the enrollment process for other coverage. You might have retiree coverage which will be secondary to Medicare, or want to purchase a Medicare Supplement and a Part D Plan or consider enrolling in a Medicare Advantage Plan. **When enrolling in any product during the Initial Enrollment Period you do not need to prove prior creditable coverage.**

9. Register on mymedicare.gov and complete the Initial Enrollment Questionnaire which tells Medicare which source of coverage is primary for you.

10. Register on any other relevant website associated with your retiree medical and drug benefits, Part D Prescription Drug Plan, Medicare Supplement or Medicare Advantage Plan.

11. If you had private, individual coverage, you almost always want to cancel it to coincide with your Medicare effective date. Do this in writing and keep a copy for your records.

12. If you are an individual who has reported more than $85,000.00 in income or a couple who has reported more than $170,000.00 in income recently to the IRS and your Medicare happens to coincide with a significant drop in income, consider completing form SSA-44, Medicare Income-Related Monthly Adjustment Amount (copy in Appendix). Discuss the form with a Social Security representative and send it in. This will allow Social Security to base your Part B and Part D premiums (if you've enrolled in Part D) on projected income rather than your income tax returns from two years ago.

13. If tax returns filed with the IRS indicate your Part B and/or Part D premiums should be income-indexed, you will receive a letter from Social Security indicating what the premiums will be. Again, individuals with a MAGI (modified adjusted gross income) over $85,000.00 and couples with a MAGI over $170,000.00 pay additional premiums. Note that the IRS is factoring in tax-exempt interest income as income for this calculation. Review this letter carefully. One client received a notice which said, "IRS told us your MAGI in 2008 was $23,188,288.00." 2008 was a good year for him (but not that good).

14. Inform all of your doctors and other medical providers of your Medicare effective date and any other coverage you have and which should pay first. Medicare is almost always primary. More than likely, you will be asked for your Medicare card.

Should everyone enroll in Part A at age 65, even those with active employer coverage?

Most people should. Like most Medicare issues, the answer to that question has become more complicated.

- If you have active group coverage through a small business, defined as fewer than 20 employees, generally you are required to be enrolled in both Medicare Parts A and B and Medicare is primary. However, some companies do not require Part B enrollment so this should be verified by your insurance company in writing.

- If you have group coverage through a larger business, defined as 20 or more employees, we would generally recommend you enroll in Part A if you've earned it. There's no reason not to have a second source of coverage if you've already paid for it. There is a major exception to this recommendation, however, which follows.

- If you have group coverage through a business and the coverage through the employer is a high deductible Plan with a health savings account, **if you want to continue to participate (make contributions or receive contributions) in the health savings account, you cannot enroll in Medicare Part A.** Health Savings Account rules can get complicated but you cannot be enrolled in Medicare and continue to contribute and use a Health Savings Account (at least under current government rules).

> *You cannot contribute, or have an employer contribute, to a health savings account if you are enrolled in Medicare Parts A or B.*

What if I don't want to enroll in Medicare?

This is a question we are occasionally asked by wealthier Americans who want to self-insure. A discussion of self-insuring is far too complicated a matter for the scope of this book. However, this section should at least help someone considering self-insuring to understand some of the risks assumed by not enrolling in Medicare.

What if I miss the Medicare Initial Open Enrollment Period at age 65?
We have seen this problem again and again. Ironically it tends to affect those fortunate enough to have retiree medical through former employment or a spouse's former employment and the retiree is oblivious to the need to enroll in Medicare.

Missing Initial Enrollment Period: Poor Timing

Jane had retiree medical through her deceased husband and knew to enroll in Medicare at age 65. She consulted with her attorney and they called Social Security the week before her birthday and learned her Part B enrollment would be delayed for a month. She had virtually no medical coverage during that time because her retiree medical was secondary to Medicare and her Medicare wasn't in place. Fortunately nothing happened to her but having had group coverage her entire life, it was extremely unnerving to have no medical coverage for a month. The situation caused so much anxiety for Jane that she altered her activity during the month to minimize any chance of injury. Because Medicare's Initial Enrollment Period is seven months long, it was not clear to her that in order to have Medicare in place as soon as she was eligible, she needed to contact Social Security during the months before her birthday.

The good news for the consumer is that the 2012 *Medicare and You* book (a mere 140+ pages) makes very, very clear that if you need to enroll in Medicare yourself, you need to do it in the months preceding your birthday. Unfortunately, on the preceding page the book reads, "If you're 65 or older, you can also apply for premium-free Part A and Part B (for which you pay a monthly premium) at www.social security.gov/retirement."

Of course, this statement is true but misleading. If you want Medicare to be in effect the month you turn 65, you need to enroll when you're 64 and before the month of your 65th birthday.

In sum, the last four months of the seven month Initial Enrollment Period are generally undesirable times to enroll. If you have to be enrolled in Medicare at age 65, best to start the process at age 64 and nine months.

Missing Initial Enrollment Period: Ignored Retiree Medical Requirements

John was a healthy 65-year-old with a younger wife who was also covered on his retiree medical. Neither realized that his former employer, like all of them, required retirees to be on Medicare as soon as they are eligible. (Frankly, in my opinion the one up-side to being bombarded by all the sales material from companies selling Supplements, Advantage Plans and Part D Plans at around age 65 results in very few people like John being oblivious to turning 65 and thinking about Medicare).

John missed both his Initial Enrollment Period and the General Enrollment Period which followed during the first quarter of every year. Unfortunately, he didn't realize his error until he received medical services one May and his retiree medical hardly paid anything because Medicare was supposed to be primary and he hadn't enrolled. That meant he could enroll in Medicare during the next General Enrollment Period but his Medicare wouldn't be effective until the following July 1 so he would have a gap in coverage of over a year.

We advised John to speak to his former employer to see if they could help him in any way. They didn't feel sorry for John and felt he should have read the benefit materials they sent him. Because John missed both his Initial Enrollment Period and his first General Enrollment Period, he will pay Part B premium penalties. In fact, he'll pay Part B premium penalties for the rest of his life. Having a gap in Medicare coverage for over a year after he tried to enroll in Medicare was a shocking, sobering and scary experience for John. He paid and will continue to pay dearly for being uninformed about Medicare's strict enrollment rules.

Missing Initial Enrollment Period: Not Living in U.S. and Not Eligible

Margaret was American but married to a foreigner. He had retiree medical through his business which was not based in the United States and she was a dependent spouse on the Plan. Neither Margaret nor her financial advisors at the time she turned 65 thought about Medicare.

Margaret was referred to us by a new financial advisor who wanted her coverage and her husband's coverage thoroughly reviewed. One issue we uncovered was that the husband's Plan had a fairly low lifetime maximum of $500,000.00 for retirees. We identified this level of coverage as inadequate and the maximum was subsequently raised to $1,000,000.00.

At the same time, Margaret was receiving expensive medical services in the United States. There were always large balance bills because the coverage provided by a Plan based outside the United States meant all care in the United States was provided on an out-of-network basis. Remember, when one is out-of-network, there is by definition no agreement in effect between your Plan and your providers and there's no obligation for charges to be reasonable. Often charges were not reasonable.

Our analysis showed Margaret would benefit from being enrolled in Medicare. She was one of those people who didn't pay into Social Security long enough to be entitled to Medicare on her own account and her husband had never worked in the U.S. As an American, however, she is allowed to "buy-in" to Medicare. In addition, she will always pay an excess premium for her Medicare Part B because she didn't sign up for Medicare during her Initial Enrollment Period. Medicare Part A penalties are different in her case. She will pay an extra 10% for every year she could have signed up but didn't and pay them for twice the number of years she could have been enrolled but wasn't. Our client could have enrolled in 2003 but didn't enroll until 2008. As a result, she will pay Part A penalties for ten years and Part B penalties for the rest of her life. **Penalties are intended for this type of situation—where someone could have but did not enroll in Medicare.**

Missing Initial Enrollment Period: Not Living in U.S. and Missed Enrollment at 65

Richard was an American married to a Canadian and they'd lived in Canada for 30 years. He qualified for premium-free Medicare Part A but chose not to enroll in Medicare Part B when he turned 65 because Canada was his primary residence. Richard later changed his mind about Part B when he and his wife wanted to keep open the option of making their U.S. home their permanent residence some time in the future.

Because Richard was a legal resident of Canada, he and his wife received coverage for medical services through the Canadian Medicare system. They also had secondary coverage through his former employer.

If Richard and his wife chose to live in their Florida home as U.S. residents, there were no good coverage options for Richard's wife. While under age 65, she couldn't get individual insurance in the private marketplace due to pre-existing conditions. When she turns 65, unlike an American who can "buy-in" to Medicare even if not eligible, this is more difficult for someone who is not an American, even for a person married to an American who has paid in to Social Security long enough to qualify for premium-free Part A. Richard's wife would have to be a legal resident of the U.S. for five years before being eligible to "buy-in" to Medicare.

Richard had enrolled in Medicare Part A during his Initial Open Enrollment but not Part B. He also missed the Initial Enrollment Period for Part D. After a great deal of discussion and consideration, Richard decided to enroll in Part B during a General Enrollment period even though the couple decided to remain in Canada as permanent residents for the time being. He pays premium penalties but knows that he is covered by Medicare Parts A and B during the months of the year he and his wife are in the U.S.

Richard decided not to enroll in Part D even though he understands that should he want to do so in the future he will pay premium penalties assessed back to May 15, 2006, the last day of Initial Enrollment for Part D.

What is Medicare's Special Enrollment Period?
This is the Enrollment Period provided to all those who continued to have ACTIVE group coverage after age 65 through their employment or a spouse's employment through businesses of 20 or more employees.

You can enroll in Medicare Parts A and B at any time while you have active group coverage. **The critical issue is that once you or your spouse stops working, you only have eight months to enroll in Part B without being subject to premium penalties and a gap in coverage. The eight month clock begins when the covered person ceases to be active or ceases to be covered by the group, WHICHEVER COMES FIRST. And, in order to avoid penalties, you must prove to Social Security that you had continuous creditable coverage back to your 65th birthday.**

> *Employers typically offer COBRA when an employee retires. COBRA is rarely a good option if you are over age 65.*

SITUATIONS THAT CREATE MEDICARE'S SPECIAL ENROLLMENT PERIOD PROBLEMS

+ Self-employed individuals with sole proprietor coverage
+ Recent retirees taking COBRA for 18 months
+ A business owner who sells his company and negotiates staying on the new owners' Health Plan without continuing in an active role
+ Executives on severance or who have a spouse who takes a severance package which includes group healthcare coverage

Most people who are working beyond age 65 and are not on Plans with health savings accounts should enroll in Medicare Part A. Then the primary issue at retirement is enrolling in Part B during a Special Enrollment Period. Part D and private Supplements have their own, different rules.

If you are an active worker or married to one, you can enroll in Part B if you'd like but you do not have to. Whether you want to typically depends on whether you think you'd use your Part B which in turn depends on your current Plan.

People make different decisions for themselves. We have a client who has never used her Part B and has a good group Plan as primary but she is a cancer survivor and wants to have as much coverage as she can. That makes her comfortable and she can afford the premiums so that's a good situation for her.

You might also consider having Part B if your Plan has a high deductible or benefit or network limitations that are unattractive to you. Employers are not supposed to discriminate against you if you are eligible for Medicare. You have every right to waive the group coverage and go on Medicare but you should also have the right to take the group Plan.

MEDICARE ENROLLMENT RULES ARE COMPLEX, PUNITIVE AND HORRIFICALLY UNFORGIVING

Medicare Part B enrollment rules are absolutely critical to understand. Worst case, if you're enrolled when you don't need to be, you're simply wasting money. However, if you miss a Part B Initial Enrollment or Special Enrollment Period, you can still get on to Medicare during an annual General Enrollment Period. But again **the General Enrollment Period is structured to impose premium penalties for life and to penalize you with a gap in Medicare coverage.**

I fear we may see more people with individual and sole proprietor coverage not enrolling in Medicare in order to avoid income-indexed Part B premiums and/or the limits doctors are putting on taking new Medicare patients. These individuals will not be eligible for a Special Enrollment Period should they ultimately decide they want to be on Medicare. They will only be able to enroll through a General Enrollment Period.

Penalties are significant. If you don't follow the rules, the government assesses a premium penalty for each year that you did not pay your Part B premiums—so back to your 65th birthday and for life.

Part B enrollment penalties probably weren't as much of a problem in the past because Part B premiums were modest. But both because of the current economy and longer life expectancy, more Americans are working after age 65 and they don't understand the rules, nor do many brokers or benefits staff. Even those who are knowledgeable about insurance tend to find Medicare confusing.

> *The Medicare and You book is a very useful resource, but it presents Part B premium penalty information in such a benign way that it's somewhat misleading.*

MEDICARE AND YOU BOOK

If you're asking yourself why you should buy and read my book when the government gives you a free *Medicare and You* book every year which is well over a hundred pages long, let me tell you. Go to Section 1 of the *Medicare and You 2012* book which discusses enrolling in Medicare Parts A and B. Here is what you'd find.

> *If you don't sign up for Part A and/or Part B (for which you pay monthly premiums) when you were first eligible, you can sign up between January 1–March 31 each year. Your coverage will begin July 1. You may have to pay a higher premium for late enrollment. See pages 28 and 30. Usually, you don't pay a late enrollment penalty if you sign up during a Special Enrollment period.*

Again, no mention of how severe the penalties are. Here's the specific language in the *Medicare and You* book regarding premium penalties:

> *If you don't sign up for Part B when you are first eligible, you may have to pay a late enrollment penalty for as long as you have Medicare* (**translation—until the day you die!**). *Your monthly premium for Part B may go up 10% for each full 12 month period that you could have had Part B, but didn't sign up for it. Usually, you don't pay a late enrollment penalty if you sign up for Part B during a Special Enrollment Period.*

If you sign up during these months:	Your coverage will begin on:
January	
February	July 1
March	

Part B Late Enrollment Penalty

If you don't sign up for Part B when you're first eligible, you may have to pay a late enrollment penalty for as long as you have Medicare. Your monthly premium for Part B may go up 10% for each full 12-month period that you could have had Part B, but didn't sign up for it. Usually, you don't pay a late enrollment penalty if you meet certain conditions that allow you to sign up for Part B during a special enrollment period. See page 23.

Example: Mr. Smith's initial enrollment period ended September 30, 2008. He waited to sign up for Part B until the General Enrollment Period in March 2011. His Part B premium penalty is 20%. (While Mr. Smith waited a total of 30 months to sign up, this included only two full 12-month periods.)

If you have limited income and resources, see page 97 for information about help paying your Medicare premiums.

Medicare and You book excerpt with
Mr. Smith enrollment and premium
penalty example.

IN MY OPINION, HERE'S WHAT THE *MEDICARE AND YOU*
BOOK SHOULD SAY IN PLAIN AND CLEAR ENGLISH

Just about everyone needs to enroll in Medicare as soon as they're eligible. For most people, that is when they're about to turn 65, ideally 64 and nine months. If you're not getting Social Security or Railroad Retirement Benefits, you need to enroll yourself through Social Security or the Railroad Retirement Board and you should do that two or three months before your 65th birthday.

You don't need to sign up for Part B if you have large group coverage (company of 20 or more employees) through your job or a spouse's job. You can choose to enroll but your Medicare will be secondary to your active group coverage. Most people with active large group coverage do sign up for Part A before they turn 65. A Special Enrollment Period is provided for those people and they have eight months after their employment ends or the group health Plan insurance based on current employment ends, **whichever happens first.** If you stay on COBRA for 18 months, have coverage through a severance agreement for an extended period of time, or sell a company and negotiate staying on the Plan as part of the sale, and don't enroll in Medicare Part B within the eight month rule, you will be very sorry. We will make you pay for that mistake forever. Your monthly premium likely will increase 10% for each full 12-month period you could have had Part B but didn't. The rules for Part D are totally different so if you make the mistake of taking COBRA and missing your Part B Enrollment Period, you still will have 63 days without penalty to enroll in Part D when your COBRA ends.

But if you missed your Initial Enrollment Period at age 65 or missed your Special Enrollment Period after you or a spouse retired from your job with coverage, you can enroll during the first quarter of every year through the General Enrollment Period. However, enrolling during the General Enrollment Period is punitive by design. You will pay the additional premiums described above for the rest of your life. Enrolling in Medicare during the General Enrollment Period is designed to be punitive in order to encourage you to enroll in Medicare Part B and pay Part B premiums as soon as you are eligible.

In addition to lifetime premium penalties, you also experience a gap in your Part B coverage for between three and 15 months which may present barriers to your getting good care and can be financially devastating as well. We certainly hope that you don't need surgery or other expensive care during the coverage gap but Medicare won't be paying for it! In sum, avoid enrolling in Medicare during the General Enrollment Period.

What if I need to enroll during a Special Enrollment Period?

Enrolling in Medicare during a Special Enrollment Period is not an honor system. Social Security wants proof you've had past coverage. Social Security relies on current and or former employer(s) to document that you have continuous coverage. You are in a Special Enrollment Period during the entire time you have coverage through your work or a spouse's through a larger employer. As a result, you can enroll in Medicare Part B at any time. The majority of our clients, most of whom will pay an income-adjusted Part B premium, plan to enroll to coincide with retirement.

Most individuals enrolling during a Special Enrollment Period already have obtained Medicare Part A during their Initial Enrollment Period. If you have not yet enrolled in Part A and want to, contact Social Security to enroll.

Social Security has very specific procedures for enrolling in Medicare Part B during a Special Enrollment Period. Here is a step-by-step guide for the Special Enrollment Period and other considerations you should take into account.

1. Decide when you want Medicare Part B to take effect. This will usually coincide with your retirement but depending on how pleased you are with your group Plan benefits, you can sign up at any time while you or a covered spouse is actively working with coverage through work. You must call Social Security to get two forms, a CMS-40B and a CMS-L564. Occasionally an employer will have these forms but generally you are on your own. Social Security will not typically forward the forms to anyone but you. For your inconvenience, these forms are not currently available on-line which is why you should request them well in advance of when you want your Medicare in place.

2. Copies of the forms are in the Appendix. As you can see, the CMS-40B is completed by the person enrolling in Medicare Part B. You must specify the requested Medicare Part B effective date. The form CMS-L564 must be completed and signed by someone from YOUR FORMER EMPLOYER(S) back to your 65th birthday to prove that you have had continuous coverage. Social Security wants original signatures from former employer(s). Obviously this can be an onerous process for those who have worked for many years beyond age 65 and might have had several employers. Note that it's possible that a former employer might be out of business which is why we advise always saving letters of creditable coverage which Social Security would accept instead of a signed form.

Plan well in advance to enroll in or change to Medicare as your primary insurance. Call the Social Security Administration for information regarding your Special Enrollment Period.

3. Be on the look-out for your new Medicare card and check to see that it has the correct Medicare Part A and B effective dates.

4. You should determine what you want in place in addition to Medicare Parts A and B and manage that enrollment process or processes. You might have retiree coverage, or want to purchase a Medicare Supplement and a Part D Plan or consider enrolling in a Medicare Advantage Plan.

5. If you are enrolling in a Medicare Supplement or Medicare Advantage Plan, you will likely have to produce the letter of creditable coverage, when available, which comes from your former insurance company after that coverage terminates, to complete enrollment in those Plans.

6. If you are enrolling in a Medicare Part D Plan, you may have to produce letters of creditable coverage or proof of coverage back to May 15, 2006, the end of Part D's first Initial Enrollment Period or your 65th birthday, whichever is more recent. You have a right to enroll within 63 days of losing your group coverage but must prove creditable coverage in order to avoid Part D premium penalties.

7. If you have not registered on mymedicare.gov you should do so. Register on any other relevant websites associated with your retiree medical and drug benefits, Part D, Medicare Supplement or Medicare Advantage Plan.

8. Call the Medicare Coordination of Benefits Department at 800-999-1118 to let them know on what date your Medicare coverage should become primary to ensure that claims are processed accordingly.

9. If your reported MAGI (Modified Adjusted Gross Income) has exceeded $85,000.00 for an individual or $170,000.00 for a couple and your income will drop below those levels in retirement, consider completing form SSA-44, Medicare Income-Related Monthly Adjustment Amount. Discuss the form with a Social Security representative, complete the form and send it in so that Social Security will base your Part B and Part D premiums on projected income rather than your income tax returns from two years ago.

10. Inform all of your doctors and other medical providers of your Medicare effective date and any other coverage you have and which should pay first. More than likely, you will be asked to produce your insurance card(s).

11. If tax returns filed with the IRS indicate that your Part B and/or Part D premiums should be income-indexed, you will receive a letter from Social Security indicating what the premiums will be. Note that the IRS is factoring in tax-exempt interest income as income for this calculation. Review this letter carefully because here's what can happen: one client received a notice which said, "IRS told us your MAGI in 2008 was $23,188,288.00." 2008 was a good year for him (but not that good). Another client's letter reads, "You had an adjusted gross income of $1,988,435.00 plus $173.00 in tax-exempt income. We added these amounts together to get your MAGI of $21,988,608.00." Fuzzy math indeed.

Prosperous Business Owner
Sells Company and Takes COBRA

Mr. Moore worked for years building a business which he finally sold at age 78. As part of his arrangement with the new owners, he decided to take COBRA for 18 months. COBRA was expensive but he'd never been on Medicare as primary and he wanted COBRA to maintain good drug coverage (Medicare Part D was not in place yet). His COBRA was going to end on March 31. Mr. Moore's family contacted us in February and we confirmed what they had been told by Social Security. Mr. Moore had missed his Special Enrollment Period. He could enroll in Medicare Part B through the General Enrollment Period but it wouldn't be effective until July 1, leaving him with a three month gap in medical coverage and Part B premium penalties assessed at 10% for every year he hadn't enrolled in Part B going back to his 65th birthday and paid for life. Staying on COBRA was a very, very costly and poor decision for Mr. Moore. We think it's scandalous. After all, he only missed contributing to Medicare Part B for the ten months he stayed on COBRA beyond the eight month Special Enrollment Rule. To be penalized for all the years back to his 65th birthday and for the rest of his life as though he were someone who decided to go without coverage and then sign up for Medicare seems excessively punitive and unreasonable.

Even more distressing was that Mr. Moore needed surgery so we addressed ourselves to the task of seeing whether we could find alternative coverage for him. He wasn't a candidate for coverage in the individual private marketplace and his state's High Risk Pool did not cover people over 65 at that time. Was he a veteran? No. If yes, that might have been a source of coverage for him. We quickly learned that he had no good options. We recommended talking to his surgeon about performing the surgery just as quickly as possible. The surgery was done and covered by Mr. Moore's COBRA. Mr. Moore was still an inpatient at the hospital when his COBRA coverage expired on March 31.

Mr. Moore was fortunate in some ways. He didn't have extremely large medical bills between March 31 when COBRA ended and July 1 when his

Medicare Part B took effect. However, it was a very stressful time and he was incredibly angry that he could face Part B premium penalties for life. It never, ever occurred to him that he would pay so dearly for taking the more expensive COBRA option.

Banking Executive
on Severance

Ed was a senior banking executive whose company had been acquired by another bank. He had been with the bank for 38 years and came to see us in the eighth month after beginning a year of severance. How companies treat severance can vary but it matters for the transition onto Medicare. I asked him, "Does the bank consider you retired for this one year of severance or does the bank consider you an active employee?" I explained that this was a critically important issue in terms of his Part B Special Enrollment. Ed was a cancer survivor. We couldn't risk any gap in coverage.

Ed told me that he had not taken a lump sum, that he was still on the regular payroll, and that this group coverage had continued on just as though he were active. His understanding was that he would be considered retired when his severance ended and that it would coincide with his eligibility for retiree medical.

There couldn't be any misunderstanding about this point so we called the bank Service Center together. I stated I had a critically important question—was Ed considered an active employee now or was he considered to be retired. If the latter, he would need to enroll in Part B immediately. The rep was quite clear that the company considered Ed to be an active employee (but excused from duties). He wasn't considered a retiree yet.

Dear Reader, I suspect now you know the terrible initial ending to this story. When it came time for this large national bank (in fact, one of the largest in the world) to complete the form to enroll Ed in Medicare Part B through his Special Enrollment Period, the information was wrong. He took the form to Social Security and tried to explain to them that the information on it was incorrect. Social Security Representatives basically said they didn't care how the company treated severance, i.e., whether he was active but excused from responsibilities or fully retired. They had rules and if the information was incorrect, then an executive of the company would have to attest that he was active and not retired within the eight months of his enrollment request.

It was no easy matter to get an executive to correct the form. Many large companies have outsourced various human resources related activities to people who have narrow expertise and little authority. Ed didn't get special attention because he had been with the company for 38 years. We finally did prevail and the company produced and signed a corrected form. Ed was enrolled in Medicare Part B without a gap but it does make you pause. We had relied on information from the company itself. It's not that they reversed course. There was just too much bureaucracy. Our advice to anyone about to take a similar severance arrangement is to discuss this thoroughly with Human Resources, clarify whether your severance period is considered active employment or not and obtain that information in writing from the company.

Retiring Executive Takes COBRA—
Hopes to Avoid Higher Part B Premiums

Jonathon was in his early 70s. He'd retired, taken COBRA and wanted to stay on it for the full 18 months so that his Part B premiums would be based on a lower income earning year. He simply didn't believe us when we said he must enroll in Part B within the eight months of no longer being active with his former company. He had the same problem others expressed—how could Medicare Part B enrollment rules, a federal program, not be in sync with one's rights under COBRA, another federal program?

One of my colleagues found a tool on mymedicare.gov which estimates Part B premiums for those who do not follow the government Special Enrollment Rules precisely. We learned that if he enrolled in Medicare during a General Enrollment Period (even though his COBRA would still be in effect), his Part B monthly premium would be $471.00 instead of the $110.00 he would otherwise pay. He was convinced and made plans to terminate his COBRA and move to Medicare and other products.

WHAT IS MEDICARE'S GENERAL ENROLLMENT PERIOD?

Medicare's General Enrollment Period is the method of last resort for enrolling in Medicare. The General Enrollment Period sounds benign but it should be avoided since it always involves premium penalties AND a gap in coverage. The General Enrollment Period is the first quarter of every year with an effective date the following July 1. If you miss March 31 (and we have dealt with many people who have), then the Medicare effective date won't be until the July 1 of the following calendar year. The General Enrollment Period is for those who either missed their Initial Enrollment or Special Enrollment Periods. To enroll in Medicare during a General Enrollment Period, call Social Security or the RRB for instructions and direction as soon as you decide you want to be enrolled in Medicare.

Medicare Part D and Enrollment Traps

What does Part D (prescription drugs) cover?

Medicare Part D covers outpatient drugs, typically pills, tablets, capsules, and injections. Drugs that are infused intravenously into the body, like chemotherapy, are covered under Part B and there are some expensive drugs that were "grandfathered" under Part B before Part D existed like blood glucose test strips and other diabetic supplies, drugs for dialysis, immunosuppressant drugs, and others.

Part D was created as part of the Medicare Modernization Act of 2003. The Initial Enrollment Period started November 15, 2005 and the program started January 1, 2006. Part D has many detractors but one has to remember that not having outpatient prescription drug coverage was an enormous dilemma for millions of people prior to 2006. Part D's coverage is often not as comprehensive as group drug coverage through a former large employer

Medicare Part D covers prescription drugs and it is administered by private companies. You must select a Plan and enroll either through Medicare or the Plan.

or union. Before 2006, however, the primary way people who did not have retiree medical purchased drug coverage was through private Medicare Supplement Plans H, I, or J. Others shopped on-line. Part D is superior to what even the richest of the Supplement Plans offered because it provides catastrophic drug coverage and often very expensive drugs are prescribed when one is diagnosed with serious illness.

Part D's unpopularity is a result of its (using insurance terminology) unusual "benefit design" which is the gap or "donut" hole. The "donut" hole is like having a deductible, i.e., no coverage, in the middle of the benefit rather than the beginning.

Who needs Medicare Part D?

In my opinion, everyone needs drug coverage so everyone should sign up for Part D, unless they have other drug coverage. You can't enroll in a Part D Plan, however, unless you are already enrolled in Medicare Part A or Part B. If you have retiree coverage through a former employer, that drug coverage is typically (but not always) better drug coverage than Part D. You should get a creditable coverage letter every year from your former employer stating whether your retiree drug coverage is creditable. Finally, if you signed up for a Medicare Advantage Plan which is an alternative to original Medicare, you need to know if the Advantage Plan has Part D benefits.

Like Medicare Parts A and B, Part D is a government benefit. However, unlike Medicare Parts A and B, Part D is administered by private companies selling Prescription Drug Plans.

Who pays for Part D?

That's a little complicated. Both taxpayers and those on Part D pay for the drug benefit. Let's discuss what the person on Part D pays.

Each person on Part D pays a premium and the premiums vary widely. You can pay as little as $15.00 per month or over $100.00 per month. Beginning in 2011, like Part B there is also an income-indexed portion of the Part D premium. The Plans have some flexibility in structuring the benefit so some Plans have a deductible and some Plans don't.

Monthly Premium—Ms. Smith pays a monthly premium throughout the year.			
1. Yearly Deductible	2. Copayment or Coinsurance (What you pay at the pharmacy)	3. Coverage Gap	4. Catastrophic Coverage
Ms. Smith pays the first $320 of her drug costs before her plan starts to pay its share.	Ms. Smith pays a copayment, and her plan pays its share for each covered drug until their **combined** amount (plus the deductible) reaches $2,930.	Once Ms. Smith and her plan have spent $2,930 for covered drugs, she is in the coverage gap. In 2012, she gets a 50% discount on covered brand-name prescription drugs and she pays 86% of the plan's cost for covered generic drugs. What she pays (and the 50% discount paid by the drug company) counts as out-of-pocket spending, and helps her get out of the coverage gap.	Once Ms. Smith has spent $4,700 out-of-pocket for the year, her coverage gap ends. Now she only pays a small coinsurance or copayment for each drug until the end of the year.

From *Medicare and You* book.

INITIAL BENEFIT PERIOD AND "DONUT" HOLE OR GAP

You are in an Initial Benefit Period at the beginning of every calendar year (or when you first enroll after a Special Enrollment Period). Until the total cost of your drugs reaches $2,930.00 in 2012 during this initial period, you and the government share in the cost of your drugs. You only pay a deductible, if you have one, and co-payments. After the initial benefit period, you lose your coverage and you're in the "donut" hole. During this period you're still paying monthly premiums and you get a discount off name-brand drugs but you're paying much more toward the full cost of your drugs.

CATASTROPHIC LEVEL

In 2012, once you reach $4,700.00 in out-of-pocket costs, meaning the deductible and co-pays you paid during the initial part of the year plus what you paid when you exhausted the initial benefit period and went into the "donut" hole (but not the premium), then you are at a catastrophic level. ACA provides a 50% discount on brand-name prescription drugs while you are in the "donut" hole. This discounted amount also counts toward reaching the catastrophic level so some aren't actually incurring $4,700.00 in out-of-pocket expense before reaching the catastrophic level. At the catastrophic level, 95% of the cost of your drugs is covered.

In sum, in 2012 a person on Part D pays a monthly premium, plus up to $4,700.00 in out-of-pocket expenses (sometimes less depending on brand-name drug discount) and 5% of cost of drugs after spending $4,700.00 out-of-pocket. Then the process starts all over again every January 1. If you transition from group coverage to Part D during the year, depending on the month you enroll in Part D, you are less likely to reach the gap or "donut" hole during that first year.

The amount one has to pay-out-of-pocket to reach the catastrophic level is adjusted upward every year. There is no cap. When you reach that level you continue to pay 5% of the cost of your drugs until a new calendar year starts the process all over again.

LOCKED-IN

There is a lock-in feature to Medicare Part D. You choose a Medicare Prescription Drug Plan (PDP) and you usually have to stay in that Plan until the following year unless you move out of your PDP service area. In 2012, you can switch one time during the year to a Medicare Advantage Plan or Medicare Prescription Drug Plan that has a 5-Star rating in your area. This is new.

From 2006 through 2010, the Annual Enrollment Period (the opportunity to change your Part D Plan) was November 15 to December 31 for an effective date of January 1. That was very undesirable because those deciding to change Plans often didn't have enough time to get their new identification cards by the time the new coverage took effect on January 1.

In 2011, the Annual Enrollment Period for Part D Plans for 2012 began on October 15 and extended to December 7 for a January 1, 2012 effective date. That is far more sensible because the Enrollment Period begins earlier and is longer so if you change Plans you are more likely to have your card well before the beginning of the year.

> *You can change Part D Plans (PDPs) every year. As of 2012 you can change once a year to a 5-Star Plan if there is one in your area.*

Does the Part D Plan you select matter?

Definitely. Again, Part D Plans are in business to make a profit. Sometimes in reviewing options, we find relatively insignificant differences among Plans in terms of cost but at times staying on your current Plan can cost you thousands of extra dollars per year. It depends totally on which prescription drugs you take.

If you are on expensive drugs or if you routinely go into the "donut" hole, you should probably review your Plan options every year.

To do a Part D review, go to mymedicare.gov/find-a-plan, and select Health and Drug Plans. If you are already on a Part D Plan, use the tool which asks you to enter personal information.

At the end of this process all the Plan choices in your geographic area will be arrayed from the least cost to the highest cost option. You don't necessarily want to choose the lowest premium Plan. You should look for a reputable, national company that is at the lower end of the cost spectrum so that you're purchasing value and a Plan that's likely to stay in business. If you don't do a Part D review, you are at higher risk of paying more than you should for drugs.

PART D AND VA DRUG BENEFITS

If you have drug coverage through the Veterans Administration, it is considered "creditable" so you can enroll in Part D at a later date without penalty. Many Veterans do enroll in both because VA formularies (list of approved drugs) can be more limited than Part D. If you have VA coverage and a Part D Plan you can't use both types of coverage for the same prescription at the same time.

What other important consideration for Part D should be taken into account?

Besides the projected cost of your drugs, there are other qualitative factors like the formulary and the rules that you should consider in selecting a Plan.

First, the formulary—this is the list of drugs the company covers. You want the drugs you take regularly to be on the formulary.

Second, the rules of the Plan often include:

+ Prior authorization: The Plan may require your doctor to provide additional information as to why you need the drug prescribed.
+ Quantity limits: The Plan limits how much medication you can get at one time.

• Step Therapy: The Plan may require you to try a generic or other cheaper medication before covering the prescribed medication.

Most people are used to dealing with quantity limit requirements. Many people are unhappy with prior authorization requirements and also resent step therapy, being forced to try a cheaper drug instead of the one their doctor prescribed. Try to select a Plan with rules you can tolerate, if possible.

OFFICIAL STATE OF RESIDENCE MATTERS

You should enroll from the state of your official residence. Medicare Part D Plans are obligated to disenroll you if they have reason to believe you no longer live in the service area where you originally enrolled. This is a headache but not one of their making. The Plans are required to do this by Medicare although this is not commonly known. To give you an example of what can go wrong, Social Security thought that our client had moved because the address Social Security had on file didn't match his Part D Plan address of record. Social Security contacted the Part D Plan and the Part D Plan in turn contacted our client to tell him that he would be disenrolled from his drug coverage within so many days. We were able to straighten this out but it required an appointment at the local Social Security office to prove our client's official residence and to demonstrate that his Plan D enrollment did coincide with that address.

We had another client who was admitted to the hospital in a nearby state while visiting her daughter. After the hospital stay, she was admitted to a nursing home. Her daughter sent a letter to the Part D Plan, a very clear letter indicating that her mother was temporarily unable to return home and requesting that any correspondence be forwarded to the daughter until further notice. You probably know what happened. The Plan acted as though the mother had moved. Even though she hadn't moved, they disenrolled her from her Part D Plan.

> *PDPs are not portable.*
> *If you move out of your immediate area,*
> *you will need to enroll in a Part D Plan*
> *near your new home.*

An important concern about these aggressive disenrollments is a failure by the person enrolled to resolve the situation if the Plan is incorrect. An elderly, frail individual on Medicare may not even see a disenrollment notice. You typically have just 63 days to enroll in a Plan if you've been legitimately disenrolled. If you miss that timeframe, you will have to wait until the next Annual Open Enrollment and could be without drug coverage for a period of time.

Of course, if you actually do move, this is the type of qualifying event which allows you to enroll in a different Part D Plan off-cycle from the Annual Open Enrollment period.

Your insurance and especially Part D should align with your state of official residence which should be consistent with the address Social Security and the IRS have on file for you.

ELIMINATING THE "DONUT" HOLE

The reform legislation—ACA—is written to ratchet down and even eliminate the "donut" hole by the end of this decade but it's impossible to know at this point what actually will happen.

HOW TO ENROLL IN MEDICARE PART D

You enroll in Medicare Part D directly through the specific Plan you want to enroll in or through Medicare via the www.mymedicare.gov website or by calling 1-800-MEDICARE, 1-800-633-4227. If you are getting retiree benefits through Social Security or the Railroad Retirement Board, you can have Part D premiums deducted from your benefit. Although you can enroll in Part D through Medicare, you never enroll in Medicare Parts A or B through Medicare. As discussed previously, that enrollment is handled by Social Security or the Railroad Retirement Board.

There is a trap associated with the Annual Open Enrollment you should know about. If you are moving from one product to another offered by the same company (many companies offer more than one option), the Plan may make your enrollment in the new Plan effective December 1 rather than January 1. Think of the negative financial impact that has on you if you've reached catastrophic level protection. At that point you are paying only 5% of the cost of your drugs. If your effective date is made earlier than January 1, your co-pays are likely to be much higher than the 5% you pay once you've reached the catastrophic level. Always check the correspondence you receive confirming your enrollment to verify the enrollment date you requested.

IRMAA—INCOME RELATED
MONTHLY ADJUSTMENT AMOUNT

Those who are expected to pay an income-adjusted Part B premium, Part D premium or both will receive a letter from Social Security referring to the information in your IRS tax returns and your income adjusted premium amounts. This is referred to as IRMAA (Income Related Monthly Adjustment Amount). We review these statements carefully for our clients and you should, too. Sometimes the process for a person new to Medicare isn't that elegant. Your premiums might be based on the standard level for most taxpayers and then adjusted upwards once Social Security receives your information from the IRS. Again, make sure you understand what level premium you should be paying.

If you're getting Social Security already, your Part B premiums are generally taken out of your Social Security payment. If you're not getting Social Security, then you are billed for your Medicare Part B premiums. The same is true for Part D although you can choose to pay the Plan directly rather than have the premiums withheld, even if you are receiving Social Security.

CREDITABLE COVERAGE ISSUES FOR BOTH PARTS B
AND D SPECIAL ENROLLMENT

Anyone who chooses to work beyond age 65 and does not enroll in Parts B and D must remember that the government for Part B or the particular Plan you enroll in for Part D will require you to provide proof of continuous creditable coverage in order to avoid what are penalties to you, but a source of revenue for the government. Insurers are obligated to send Letters of Creditable Coverage to anyone whose coverage is terminated by a Plan but many people don't understand the importance of those letters or the need to keep them with their other important records.

Let's be very, very clear about this. If you work to age 80 and need to enroll in Medicare Part B during a Special Enrollment Period, Social Security will want paperwork signed by a representative of each employer you had back to the month you turned 65 to determine that you had no break in coverage. Part D Plans will be looking for proof that you had drug coverage back to May 15, 2006, the last day of the Initial Enrollment Period for the first year of Part D or the month and year you turned 65, whichever is more recent.

PART D SPECIAL ENROLLMENT PROBLEMS

Our client was a teacher still working at age 70 and covered by the school's large group Plan when he suffered a stroke. The school's benefits allowed him to stay on the group Plan as primary for up to one year after his stroke. He was already enrolled in Medicare Part A and shortly after the stroke, enrolled in Medicare Part B. After the year, if he wasn't able to return to work or chose not to, he would transition to Medicare as primary. The school did not offer any retiree medical.

The year passed and he wasn't returning to work so he needed to enroll in a Medicare Part D Plan. He had to prove that he had had creditable drug coverage back to May 15, 2006, the last day of Initial Open Enrollment in Part D. Fortunately, he had only had one employer, the school, during this period but there had been two different insurance carriers. We had to get the documentation from 2006 and 2007. Quite understandably, our client hadn't saved any information regarding his former New Jersey-based Plan. The school couldn't help us except to indicate the name of the insurance company since they didn't have a business relationship with the Plan any longer. We didn't even have the identification number which was in effect while he had that coverage so it wasn't an easy matter to obtain proof of the client's former coverage. We persisted and were able to get proof of his coverage but it was a tedious, laborious process. This is another reason you should always keep your creditable coverage paperwork.

Another problem with Part D Special Enrollment is Part D Plans enrolling you in advance of the requested effective date of coverage. It is remarkable that the Center for Medicare Services and Medicaid Services allows this. Here's the scam. You are retiring effective December 31 and have good group coverage including prescription drugs through that date. You apply for a Medicare Prescription Drug Plan for January 1 and receive confirmation of that date through your on-line enrollment application done through medicare.gov. However, Medicare is allowing Plans to enroll you on December 1 so that you have a month of double coverage for prescription drugs for which you pay an extra month's premium to the PDP but continue to use your group coverage benefits. Here is the wording from a client enrollment done through the medicare.gov Enrollment Center:

> *Enrollment can be effective as early as the first of the next month depending on your circumstances. The Plan you have selected will inform you of your effective date of enrollment.*

Have you followed me? Medicare is allowing an earlier enrollment than you requested so that your PDP receives an extra month's premium while you continue to use your other coverage. It is outrageous. The best way to protect yourself from this situation is to avoid enrolling until the month preceding your desired effective date.

MEDICARE.GOV

We strongly recommend that as soon as you enroll in Medicare, even if it's initially just Medicare Part A, you register on the website www.mymedicare.gov. The tools on this website keep getting better. Some clients have said, "I don't want my information on the internet." Well, it's on the internet so it's best to check to see that the information is accurate.

On mymedicare.gov, you can determine if Medicare has correct information about your secondary coverage, you can verify if Medicare has correct information on which coverage is primary, and you can view claim information as well.

You can usually verify your enrollment in Medicare through the website before getting your Medicare card and it's often a relief to see that you are enrolled. Again, mymedicare.gov, is a very good tool and everyone should take advantage of it.

> www.mymedicare.gov
> is a very useful tool. Register with the site
> as soon as possible to verify that information
> about your coverage is accurate and
> to view benefits and claims.

Medicare Supplements

P rivate Medicare Supplements or so-called Medi-Gap Plans (these terms are synonymous) are private products that pay deductibles and coinsurance after Medicare Part A or B pays. If you have original Medicare and the typical array of Medicare and Medicare-related products, you'll have Medicare Parts A, B, a Part D Plan and often a private insurance Supplement. Some choose not to have a Supplement and we'll discuss that later, too. The premiums for a private Supplement, unlike Parts B or D or Medicare Advantage Plans can never be deducted from a government benefit because they are private Plans sold by insurance companies. You must always pay the insurance company directly for that coverage.

As mentioned before, traditional Medicare is structured like the major medical Plans of the 1960s. As a result, there are deductibles and co-insurance for most services. You almost always have out-of-pocket costs when you use Medicare services. If you are admitted to a hospital in 2012, the Medicare Part A deductible is $1,156.00. If you see a doctor who accepts Medicare assignment which is similar to a doctor who is in-network in a non-Medicare Plan, Medicare pays 80% of their approved charge and you pay 20% (more to follow under Doctors).

Medicare Supplements or
Medi-gap Plans are private products
(not a government benefit).

If you have good retiree coverage secondary to Medicare, you generally don't need to consider purchasing a Supplement. You might buy one to have the catastrophic hospitalization coverage a Supplement provides, explained later. Your objective should always be to be well insured but being over-insured can be a waste of money. Years ago a new client came to us who for 25 years paid for an expensive Medicare Supplement that included drug coverage and she was eligible for TRICARE as the widow of a retired military person. It was such a shame since she hadn't ever used her TRICARE benefits and the drug benefits in TRICARE were far superior to those in her Supplement and later in her Medicare Part D. She wasted tens of thousands of dollars to purchase inferior coverage compared to what TRICARE offered.

How many different Medicare Supplements are there?

There are probably too many Supplement choices in most states. For many years, Plans A through J were available in most states but in the past several years, K and L and M and N were added and E, H, I and J were removed. It actually made sense that some were removed because H, I and J had drug coverage in them. This was before Medicare Part D took effect in 2006. As a result, since 2006, Plan J and Plan F were almost identical anyway. Unfortunately it can be a great source of anxiety to learn that the Supplement you've had for many years has been eliminated but anyone who already had one of these Plans has been grandfathered.

In some states there are also so-called Medicare Select Supplement options. Medicare Select products have the same benefits as their associated products but cost less because there is a more limited network of providers.

We have included in the Appendix a graph which shows the various Plan options and what they cover. Often this information can be found on your State Insurance Department website in one format or another. Just a few years ago when there were Plans A through J, it was easy to explain that A was the least comprehensive Plan and J the most comprehensive. But since then, H, I and J have been removed and Plans K,L, M and N have been added, so you have to be careful.

Which is the most comprehensive Plan?

Plan F, in the 47 states where it is available, is the most comprehensive. It pays 100% of Medicare Part A and B services after Medicare pays. There is also a high deductible Plan F although fewer insurance companies offer it. With the high deductible Plan F, you currently pay the first $2,000.00 in out-of-pocket expenses and then the Plan coverage kicks in paying 100%

after Medicare Part A and Part B pay. The federal government is considering a surcharge to those on regular Plan F under the theory that those whose entire out-of-pocket costs are covered through a Plan they've purchased will use unnecessary medical services. It's too early to know the fate of that proposal.

Massachusetts and Minnesota offer two Supplement choices and Wisconsin offers a basic Plan with several optional riders.

> *In most states, one can choose among Medicare Supplements, A, B, C, D, F, K, L, M, or N. Massachusetts, Wisconsin and Minnesota have fewer choices.*

Do any Supplements contain drug coverage?
Not if they were purchased after 2005. Private Supplements H, I and J had drug coverage until 2006 when Medicare Part D was passed. Medicare Supplements sold since the end of 2005 do not include drug coverage.

How are Private Medicare Supplement Plans regulated?
It is extremely important to remember that Medicare Supplements are regulated by both the federal government and state governments. It is also important to remember that several key issues vary by state.

FEDERAL OVERSIGHT—STANDARDIZED BENEFITS
The federal government determines what benefits are covered in a given Supplement. That means that a Plan F provided by one company has the EXACT SAME benefits as a Plan F provided by another company anywhere in the United States. The same is true of a Plan A or a Plan N. The benefits are the same regardless of what company provides the coverage and what they charge for it. Since the benefits are the same, you do not want to overpay for your Supplement.

Federal regulations also require that an agent or broker cannot sell a Supplement without the client understanding that the client should not have more than one Supplement. Private Supplements do not "coordinate" benefits meaning they are secondary to Medicare and there is no advantage to having more than one Supplement. Years ago we were retained by an attorney to review her client's healthcare coverage portfolio. Unfortunately, her client had three Medicare Supplements and a variety of other rather worthless discount programs she had joined, but she could not benefit from all of them. All these companies had her credit card and were renewing everything automatically. This is just the type of situation federal regulation is intended to prevent at least with respect to Medicare Supplements.

> *You could be paying too much for your Medicare Supplement. Comparison shop for information on Plans and associated premiums.*

STATE INSURANCE DEPARTMENTS AND STATE DIFFERENCES

State Insurance Departments also regulate Medicare Supplements in several key ways and they are an excellent source of information. You typically go to your state's Insurance Department website, click on Consumer, then Health, then Medicare and review what the various topics are. Many sites have information on every company that sells Supplements in that state, which Supplements they offer, the approved premium and a contact telephone number.

My home state, Connecticut, shows one graph of all the federally approved Supplements, A through N, (less E, H, I and J which have been eliminated), and what they cover. Another chart shows the approved companies in the state and the approved premiums for each Plan. Both of these charts are in the Appendix to this book to show you the kind of information you want to find. As you will see, as of September 2011 in Connecticut, you could pay as low as $210.50 and as high as $420.37 per month for a Plan F premium. That same month you could buy a Plan A Supplement for as low as $122.75

or as high as $526.93 per month. Remember a Plan A Supplement has the same benefits as any other Plan A Supplement. A Plan A Supplement provides far less comprehensive coverage than a Plan F Supplement. Anyone in Connecticut paying $526.93 for a Plan A Supplement is wasting a great deal of money because a more comprehensive Plan A Supplement can be purchased for a lower premium from a different company for far less.

PREMIUMS WHICH CAN BE CHARGED

In fact, reviewing premiums by company or insurer across states can be fascinating. In general, insurance premiums will be higher in higher cost areas of the country but how the state's Insurance Department regulates the companies offering these products differs and matters. As the chart with Connecticut premiums reveals, the state of Connecticut, which is small with just over three million people, is handled as one insurance marketplace. Contrast this with Westchester County, New York, the adjacent county to our west, which has two premium structures within the county, a higher premium for the more expensive southern portion of the county and a lower premium for the less expensive medical marketplace, northern Westchester. Westchester has a population of just under one million.

Yes, you can definitely overpay for your Medicare Supplement. Over the years we have also encountered a number of "deals" that have been made to offer Supplements to particular groups, usually a medical or dental society. We have yet to see a good one but there's always hope. At any rate, it makes sense to be a prudent purchaser and not pay more than you should.

RATE STRUCTURE

Geography can be one element of rate structure but age and whether or not you are a smoker matter depending on the state you live in. As you can see from Connecticut's chart, whether you are 65 or 105, you will pay the same premium. Other states have five year rate bands so that at age 70, age 75, age 80, etc. you pay higher rates.

Idaho, at least for the time being, has one year rate bands so in addition to any premium increase for the year, at each birthday you're paying a relatively higher rate. As a result, you pay less if you're 65 than if you're 85.

In other states like Maryland and Florida, there is a non-smoker premium and a smoker premium. Again, state environments vary with respect to how premiums are established for Medicare Supplements.

PURCHASING A MEDICARE SUPPLEMENT

During an Initial Enrollment Period or a Special Enrollment Period, when you are transitioning onto Medicare Part B, you have a six month Medicare Supplement Open Enrollment Period to purchase any Supplement. After that six month period expires, your opportunity to purchase a Supplement depends to a great extent on your state of residence.

Remember that Enrollment Periods are simply windows of time within which you must act on a matter related to insurance or suffer the consequences. As a result, when you apply for a Medicare Supplement during an official Enrollment Period, you typically don't even answer any questions related to your health. Your health status is irrelevant.

If you go onto Medicare due to disability, you also can go on a Medicare Supplement in many states but depending on your state, your choice of Plans might be limited. Federal law does not require insurance companies to sell Supplement Plans to people under 65.

Some states allow insurers to medically underwrite Medicare Supplements applied for outside an Enrollment Period and to deny the application based on health status. Medical underwriting means that when you apply for the insurance product you are given a list of questions to answer much like the questions you are asked when you go to a new doctor. With insurance that is "medically underwritten" as opposed to "guaranteed issue," if you answer "yes" to too many questions, your application may be denied. In essence, if the insurer believes you are too great a risk, they are likely to lose money on you, and they often have no obligation (again, this depends on your state of residence) to extend coverage to you.

If you don't have another source of coverage secondary to Medicare and you decide not to obtain a Supplement during an Enrollment Period, you should know the rules about medical underwriting in your state.

WAITING PERIODS

This issue varies significantly by state. In New York, all Supplements can be purchased on a guaranteed issue basis outside of an Enrollment Period at any time. However, all Plans can impose a six month waiting period during which they don't have to pay any of the expense associated with a pre-existing condition. They may contest all significant claims that come to them during that six month period.

Across the border in Connecticut, whether or not to impose a pre-existing condition exclusion and the length of a pre-existing condition exclusion—the waiting period—is left to the discretion of the company offering the

Plan. Some Plans have no waiting period, some have one month, some two months, three months and six months. You need to understand what is available in your state.

CATASTROPHIC HOSPITALIZATION

An increasingly important issue is catastrophic hospitalization coverage, a benefit offered in private Medicare Supplements and Medicare Advantage Plans. ACA may require more Retiree Medical Plans to offer catastrophic hospitalization coverage when Medicare Part A benefits are exhausted. The Medicare Catastrophic Coverage Act of 1988 was repealed in 1989. That Act provided unlimited hospitalization benefits to those on Medicare. The Act was unpopular because the cost of the program was passed on to those on Medicare rather than being more widely subsidized by all taxpayers like so much of Medicare is.

A Supplement contains an extra 365 days of hospitalization coverage beyond what Medicare Part A provides and we have seen numerous instances where Medicare Part A has been exhausted. The cruel reality of our times is that we can live longer lives in impaired conditions which in prior times we wouldn't have survived.

> *Medicare Part A covers up to 150 days of hospitalization and/or skilled nursing. When you haven't used Part A for 60 days, the first 90 of the 150 days replenishes. Your 60 Lifetime Reserve Days never replenish.*

How does Medicare Part A (hospitalization coverage) work?
Each person on Part A has a benefit of 150 hospital days, 60 of which are so-called lifetime reserve days and they are aptly named. If you use them, they never replenish.

When you are admitted to a hospital or subsequent nursing or rehabilitation facility, the clock starts on your Part A benefits. A simple example would be using 90 straight days of hospitalization. If you were then able to go home or be "facility free" for 60 days in a row (not using your Part A at all), your 90 day benefit totally replenishes.

It's not common but patients can be hospitalized for 90 straight days. It is more typical that someone goes from hospital to skilled nursing to home and then is readmitted and may go back and forth but is never "facility free" for 60 consecutive days. Everyone should know that if you go beyond 90 Medicare Part A hospital days and they don't replenish, you're using your 60 remaining lifetime reserve days which never replenish. Should you exhaust those and be in a hospital and unable to be discharged home or unable to be "facility free" for 60 days, you will have to pay unless you have a private Supplement, Advantage Plan, or some other form of hospital coverage secondary to Medicare.

Exhausting hospitalization coverage can result in hospital bills of hundreds of thousands of dollars. We have seen them.

Couple with Retiree Medical; Wife Exhausts Part A

Mr. and Mrs. Hart thought they had excellent retiree benefits. After all, Mr. Hart had worked for his former employer, a *Fortune* 100 company, for almost his entire adult life. They had never had a problem with significant medical bills. As they got older, both Mr. and Mrs. Hart's health seriously deteriorated and Mrs. Hart had major system failures over the course of two years. They didn't notice the Medicare Summary Notice which indicated that Mrs. Hart had used all 60 of her Lifetime Reserve Days. She remained in the Hospital.

After Mrs. Hart died, the estate received a bill from the local hospital for $800,939.00 for the period after her Medicare was exhausted and the secondary coverage reached its lifetime maximum. No one from the Hospital's billing department or social work department had informed the couple or family during this period that in their state Mrs. Hart could have purchased a Medicare Supplement without a waiting period to obtain additional hospital coverage, since the retiree coverage did not include catastrophic hospitalization. That wasn't their job.

An interesting point related to this tragedy is that the ACA requires the removal of limits on hospitalization which might have protected this family. However, I fear employers will see these new unlimited benefits as a potential risk they don't want to assume and will restructure or eliminate retiree medical benefits in order to reduce their exposure.

Widow Overpaying
for Medicare Supplement

Mrs. Martin's deceased husband had purchased a Medicare Supplement for both of them through a medical association. After he passed away, she didn't think to question whether she was overpaying for the Supplement. While assisting Mrs. Martin with another matter, we learned what she was paying for her Supplement and informed her she could pay $200.00 less a month for exactly the same coverage through a reputable insurance company. Mrs. Martin changed her Plan.

Medicare Advantage

Medicare Advantage (formerly referred to as Part C or Choice+) Plans are alternatives to original Medicare managed by private companies. Medicare gives the money they estimate would be spent on you that year to the private company you select. Historically most Plans were HMOs (Health Maintenance Organizations) but PPOs (Preferred Provider Organizations), and the newer PFFS (Private Fee for Service Plans) are also available.

> *Medicare Advantage Plans*
> *are private Plans which are an alternative*
> *to original Medicare.*

LOCKED-IN

Like Medicare Part D, with a Medicare Advantage Plan you are locked-in to your choice, generally for a year unless you move to another area. New in 2012 is the option to make one change per year to a 5-Star Plan if there is such a Plan in your area. Medicare Advantage Plans historically have presented the same choice as other managed care products. You might pay less for your benefit package and in exchange you agree to a network and more "rules" like pre-authorization requirements that non-Medicare Plans have. Whether or not Medicare Advantage Plans are attractive depends entirely on where you live, your physicians and your values and priorities.

PROVIDER NETWORK

You should be careful to understand the provider network in a Medicare Advantage Plan. A client came to us having joined an Advantage Plan for the lower costs when he was totally healthy. Then during the year he was diagnosed with a very aggressive cancer. He wanted to go to Memorial Sloan Kettering for treatment but Sloan Kettering was not in the network. If he went to Sloan Kettering as a Medicare Advantage member with that Plan, he was going to have to pay cash. There was NO coverage. Had he been on original Medicare, being treated at Sloan would have been covered.

There are PPO Advantage Plans available now where you enjoy much of the freedom of original Medicare where you can choose which doctors and providers you want to see. These Plans have co-pays at varying levels for most services so they're fairly good choices for people who won't use too many services.

INFORMATION ON MEDICARE ADVANTAGE PRODUCTS

Often there is good information on your State Insurance Department's website. Click on "consumer," then "health," then "Medicare" to see what information is there.

Another good source of information is the *Medicare and You Book* which the federal government prints every year for everyone on Medicare. *Medicare and You* contains a great deal of useful information but it's over 100 pages and full of terms many people don't understand. Nevertheless, the end of the book is customized by geographic area to show the various Medicare Advantage Plans available where you live. You can also view this information on-line. If you don't receive a copy by mail, you can call Social Security and request a copy. Copies may also be available at your local Social Security office.

WHEN ARE MEDICARE ADVANTAGE PRODUCTS NOT A GOOD CHOICE?

It's important to understand that Medicare Advantage Plans are specifically tied to a geographic area as a result of federal regulation. We have had numerous calls from people whose parents were on a Medicare Advantage product in Florida but once they became very elderly and sick, they couldn't remain in Florida. One misunderstood that moving out of Florida enabled her to switch back to original Medicare. She remained on her Florida Advantage Plan and sought care from several expensive New York specialists. She didn't understand that her Florida Plan would only cover "urgent and emergent" care outside of Florida and had to pay cash to all those doctors. Also, she wasn't eligible to remain on the Florida Advantage Plan once she moved. When she moved from Florida to New York, the move was a qualifying event enabling her to return to either original Medicare or to join another Medicare Advantage Plan.

Another was visiting a relative and had a precipitous decline in health. The family determined he could not return to Florida. They sought our help so that the transition back to original Medicare could occur at the first of the next month but the claims from the prior three weeks ended up being disputed as "urgent and emergent" by the Florida Plan.

An adult daughter wanted her mother to move out of Florida to be closer to her and to be able to return to original Medicare but didn't want the mother to lose her official Florida residence where there is no income tax. I explained to her that we couldn't fill that tall order since only an official move out of the state would allow her to disenroll from the Florida Advantage Plan and return to original Medicare. If she maintained her Florida residence as her official residence, she would have to wait until the Annual Enrollment Period to transition from her Advantage Plan back to traditional Medicare.

If you have more than one home, Medicare Advantage products are often not a good choice since only urgent and emergent care is covered outside the service area associated with the individual's primary residence. Medicare Advantage products are not a good choice for someone who isn't going to put forth the effort to truly understand the benefits, the network, the rules and might have "remorse" at being locked in to a Plan.

In spite of all these reservations, Medicare Advantage Plans can be an excellent choice if you've belonged to a reputable Plan with a long history or live in an area where this is a reputable Plan. **What gets lost in the debate with respect to Medicare Advantage Plans is that there are high quality Medicare Advantage Plans that have been in business for many years.** They should be viewed very differently from the Plans we read about in the newspapers, those that have been sanctioned repeatedly for their aggressive, unscrupulous agents who enroll unwitting seniors who have no idea what they've signed up for.

ENROLLING IN MEDICARE ADVANTAGE PLANS

You can enroll in a Medicare Advantage Plan during your Initial Enrollment Period to coincide with going on Medicare at age 65. Between October 15 and December 7 you can join, switch or drop a Medicare Advantage Plan for a January 1 effective date. Between January 1 and February 14, if you are in a Medicare Advantage Plan, you can leave and change back to original Medicare. If you do so, you have until February 14 to enroll in a Medicare Part D Plan.

MEDICARE ADVANTAGE SUMMARY

All Plans are not the same. You should understand the pros and cons before selecting a Plan. Know that it is illegal for a Plan to contact you via telephone which is why there is so much mail to those who are eligible at enrollment times.

Regardless of your interest in enrolling in a Medicare Advantage Plan, you should understand what Medicare Advantage Plans are. Some companies are in the Medicare Advantage business, the Medicare Part D business and the Medicare Supplement business. You should never be in a Medicare Advantage Plan and have a private Medicare Supplement which Supplements traditional Medicare. We have dealt with people who enrolled without realizing what they enrolled in. That shouldn't happen. Of course today's healthy 65 year-old may be very capable in terms of understanding these issues. A frail 85 year-old or the adult daughter of the frail 85 year-old may not have any ability to do so and the mail during Enrollment Periods from companies offering these Plans can be overwhelming, confusing, and scary.

Anyone considering enrolling in a Medicare Advantage Plan for the first time should carefully evaluate the Plan relative to the other options available to them. At the same time, if someone has been in a Medicare Advantage Plan for decades and has been happy with it and the doctors are still in the Plan, probably best to let things be. We have seen adult children of 90 something year old parents who after decades have realized their parent is in what they describe as a Medicare HMO and they are horrified. They want the parent out. Individuals who've been well served by a Plan for many years, have enjoyed good relationships with their doctors and appreciate features like not getting paperwork associated with every claim often should likely be left in the Plan unless there is a compelling reason to change.

Retiree Benefits

etiree medical benefits are medical and prescription drug benefits provided to those who have worked for a company or union long enough to earn them upon retirement. Retiree medical benefits are a critical protection for those who have retired before age 65. For those 65 and over for whom Medicare is primary, however, we often see benefits that aren't as valuable as they used to be. This is due to the ever increasing cost of medical benefits. In addition, since Medicare Part D was added in 2006, it is easier for companies to decide to discontinue retiree benefits for those on Medicare. Before 2006, Medicare had no outpatient prescription drug program. ACA presents other threats to employers maintaining retiree medical due to the increased benefits included in that legislation.

If you've retired prior to age 65 and have postponed taking your social security or Railroad Retirement Benefits, then you MUST actively enroll in Medicare Parts A and B (and D if your retiree medical doesn't offer drug benefits) two or three months before your 65th birthday. Your former employer requires that you are enrolled in Medicare. By enrolling at the beginning of your Initial Enrollment Period, your Medicare coverage will be in effect as soon as you are eligible. Medicare will be primary and your retiree medical will be your secondary source of medical coverage.

Once you're on Medicare, enroll on mymedicare.gov and complete Medicare's Initial Enrollment Questionnaire to communicate to Medicare that it will be primary. Track over time that the information on mymedicare.gov is correct.

> *ACA adds higher risk to Retiree Medical Plans because various benefits now have to be unlimited. Be aware. Your Plan may change, be restructured or eliminated to avoid this added risk.*

How do you know how good your retiree benefits are?
Often with great difficulty if you are 65 or older.

The value of your retiree coverage is the combination of what benefits are covered and what you're paying for those benefits versus what's available to you with either a Medicare Supplement, Advantage Plan and/or Part D Plan. It has never been more important to know, and in many instances it has never been more difficult to know, the value of your retiree coverage. At the same time, it is almost always a very stressful decision to decline retiree benefits because you typically can't re-enroll once you decide to leave the Plan.

We see the full spectrum of situations:

+ The former employer offers retiree benefits that are subsidized and of wonderful value to the retiree
+ The former employer essentially extends the benefits at the employer's cost
+ The employer is charging a ridiculous amount for the benefits offered compared to what's available in the private marketplace
+ The value of retiree benefits continues to erode, sometimes slowly, sometimes quickly

When the employer is charging an amount beyond what seems reasonable, we feel it is almost kinder for the former employer to eliminate retiree medical rather than have people overpay for benefits because they're afraid to drop them or because they are incapable of evaluating the situation. For example, we once met with a new client who was paying substantially more for his retiree dental premium than the annual benefit would pay which plainly makes no sense at all.

PRESCRIPTION DRUG BENEFITS WITH RETIREE MEDICAL

Because of the "donut" hole in Medicare Part D, retiree drug benefits are almost often better coverage for drugs than Part D. That is a main reason so many people, especially on expensive medications or with a spouse on expensive medications, would choose to keep their retiree medical. We haven't seen many Plans continue to offer retiree medical and suspend their drug benefits but there are some and this may be an increasing trend if Medicare Part D benefits become more attractive.

In analyzing the value of retiree medical benefits compared to options, it is often a mixed bag. The retiree medical coverage may not be as good for those 65 and over or may be more expensive than a private Medicare Supplement. Typically, however, the retiree drug benefits are superior to Medicare Part D drug benefits.

HIGH DEDUCTIBLES

Retiree Plans with higher deductibles are becoming more and more common. Let's say your Plan has a $2,000.00 deductible per person per year. If you're relatively healthy, then often your retiree coverage isn't paying for any medical expenses until perhaps the very end of the year. If you need surgery or a major procedure, then hopefully you'll have it in the beginning of the year so that you're meeting that deductible and getting some coverage from your Plan earlier in the year. It's often worth keeping a Plan like this but it depends entirely on how much you are paying for it compared to how much you might pay for products in the Medicare marketplace, like the combination of a private Medicare Supplement and a Part D Plan.

FEE SCHEDULE

Sometimes it is difficult to know how good the retiree Plan is until one is on it because retiree materials will say "we pay according to a fee schedule" but there is no information about where the fee schedule is set. There are so many procedures and codes paid that it's not considered a simple request to ask for the fee schedule although you can ask. At times the fee schedule is so low that the Plan rarely pays anything after Medicare Part A or B even after the deductible is met. As a result, with a reasonably healthy retiree it would be almost impossible for the employer to incur much expense other than drug for the retiree or spouse because the Plan isn't paying anything after Medicare Part A or B pays or isn't paying much.

How can you tell how rich the Plan might be?

It's extremely difficult to tell until you see how claims are actually processed. The fee schedule for Part B claims may be set like a Plan F Supplement so that the entire balance after Medicare has paid is covered. It may be set to pay 80% after Medicare pays. That's a good benefit but somewhat of a hassle because it means you often will owe very small balances after Medicare pays and after your secondary coverage pays. Sometimes the fee schedule is set below what Medicare pays so you owe the entire balance after Medicare pays.

I have only seen one retiree Benefits Booklet EVER that was refreshingly direct with respect to the fee schedule. It said "we rarely pay after Medicare Part A or Part B pays." The Plan had a $700.00 deductible. The Plan language indicates that the fee schedule has been set around or even below the Medicare fee schedule. As a result, that's pretty clear—the value of that retiree Plan is primarily in the drug coverage. In that kind of situation some would choose to have a private Medicare Supplement and some would not depending on their circumstances and whether they lived in a state where they could always purchase a Supplement later.

Can you get good information from your benefits department?

Sometimes but my advice would be to not count on getting good advice from your company's Human Resource or Benefits staff if you are a retiree 65 or over. Let's be realistic. The primary responsibility for those dealing with Benefits in a large company is the active work force. Most Benefits Department staff would acknowledge that it is beyond the scope of their responsibilities to understand the complexities of Medicare. They certainly have no obligation to learn about the alternatives a retiree might have should the retiree want to consider declining the retiree coverage and go on Medicare products instead.

SURVIVOR BENEFITS

Survivor benefits mean that the retiree benefits are extended to the spouse should the retiree die first. Trying to find out whether there are survivor benefits can be difficult, too. It's preferable to know in advance if a retiree Plan includes survivor benefits so you can plan accordingly. It's terrible enough to be a new widow but many without survivor benefits get a letter of condolence which also reads that "you are off the coverage at the end of the month" unless you elect COBRA. COBRA is rarely a good option for people over age 65 and yet companies have to extend COBRA benefits to comply with federal regulations.

> *Spouses of individuals with Retiree*
> *Medical Coverage must know if benefits*
> *will continue should that spouse die first.*
> *If not, the surviving spouse has 63 days*
> *to find new coverage.*

RETIREE MEDICAL FROM A FORMER EMPLOYER—
WHEN TO CALL IT QUITS

It can be a very difficult and trying decision to eliminate retiree benefits. For our client, described below, however, the former employer made it an easier decision than is typical. Our client, a widow, was paying $558.00/month in 2005 for excellent retiree medical benefits through the company her husband had chaired. This was a high premium but the Plan had excellent drug benefits and Medicare Part D had not yet started. Then on December 16, 2005 she received a letter as part of open enrollment that the company had been charging incorrectly and she should have been charged much more for her retiree healthcare coverage. Fortunately for her, so the letter said, they would not be asking for a refund associated with prior years.

The letter went on to say that the new monthly charges for health insurance would be $1,451.00, more than two-and-a-half times the level of expense she'd paid that year. This meant she would be paying $17,412.00 per year for coverage secondary to Medicare. We got in touch with the widow's husband's former company and were given permission to speak to the company's broker. What the company had decided to do was to charge the same amount for retirees who were under 65 for whom the company's Plan would pay first and retirees over age 65 for whom Medicare would pay first.

This may have been the first time that we ever recommended that someone give up retiree medical but it was an easy recommendation to make. The cost of a Plan F Supplement which pays the entire balance after Medicare pays was about $200.00/month at that time. Part D was going to be available on January 1 and our client was taking two prescription medications both of which were generic and inexpensive. Even if she had enrolled in Part D and gone through the "donut" hole, she would have spent $4,500.00 to reach the catastrophic level in 2006.

We advised that she get a Medicare Plan F Supplement, enroll in Medicare Part D and take COBRA for 18 months, the COBRA being in place solely for the limited dental benefit. She was already enrolled in Medicare Parts A and B. It would have been kinder if the company had just terminated the coverage.

Sometimes you have an iron-clad guarantee to your benefits because of a court decision, for example, or a union contract. But in the U.S., that's rarely the case for non-union employees. In fact, the opposite is often true. Corporate takeovers can allow the new entity to eliminate retiree benefits for all those who were once eligible. We've seen this in many instances, including with the former CEO of a U.S. steel company.

THE FUTURE OF RETIREE MEDICAL BENEFITS

Although certainly there will be exceptions, today's retiree over age 65 who has rich retiree medical benefits should probably anticipate changes in their benefits. You have to be realistic. The ACA adds more risk to employers and Plans by removing lifetime maximums. Some employers will act to limit that risk. You cannot assume that a good Plan today will be a good Plan in the future. Many corporations would love to be out of the business of offering rich retiree medical and having to list that liability on their balance sheets. One client's company recently eliminated all retiree medical benefits and will offer retirees an annual stipend of $2,200.00 toward coverage they enroll in as individuals. This change vastly reduces the company's financial risk.

Pay very close attention to changes in your retiree medical benefits. It may not be necessary to review them carefully every year if the benefits seem stable but I would always recommend that at least every few years you should make a concerted effort to determine if the benefits have diminished and, if so, how.

Doctors

A
nother issue when transitioning onto Medicare is the new language describing how physicians participate in the Medicare Program. The non-Medicare language of in-network and out-of-network is replaced with accepting assignment, not accepting assignment or opting out of Medicare. You want to know which category your doctors fall into.

ACCEPTING MEDICARE ASSIGNMENT

A doctor who accepts Medicare assignment is fairly analogous to a doctor who is in-network in the non-Medicare world. The doctor submits a claim to Medicare and Medicare "assigns" the payment directly to the doctor, meaning the doctor's office is paid directly. If you have a Medicare Supplement or retiree medical as a secondary source of coverage, typically an electronic link called a Part B cross-over is set up so that Medicare claim information goes to the secondary carrier electronically without your having to file a claim. This is a wonderful convenience. Then the secondary carrier pays its portion of the claim. The amount paid depends entirely on the coverage you have. If there's still a balance, you then pay that.

Doctors who accept assignment have agreed to receive 80% of the amount Medicare allows doctors to charge for that service, or the Medicare fee schedule. If Medicare's approved fee is $100.00, the doctor's office would be paid $80.00 from Medicare, for example. If you have a Plan F Supplement, the remaining $20.00 would be paid by the Supplement. If you had no secondary coverage, you would owe the $20.00.

Doctors who accept assignment cannot charge whatever they want. Their charges are dictated by the government and over the years what the government pays has become lower and lower, which is why more physicians, especially primary care physicians, are unhappy with reimbursement from Medicare and also why some have opted out of Medicare altogether.

NOT ACCEPTING MEDICARE ASSIGNMENT OR "UNASSIGNED" CLAIMS

The term "not accepting Medicare assignment" is very unfortunate because it sounds as though the physician may not have any relationship with the Medicare program. That's not true. Here's how it works.

When you see a doctor who does not accept assignment, he or she can charge up to 15% more than the Medicare approved charge. Also, the office can ask you for that payment at the time of service but many do not.

The office of the doctor who does not accept assignment also submits the claim to Medicare but the payment comes to you. In fact, Medicare Summary Notices (the Medicare equivalent of a non-Medicare Explanation of Benefit form or "EOB") are always separated by assigned and unassigned claims. An unassigned claim will have a check to tear off. Consumers rarely file claims with Medicare. When they do it is usually to get a Medicare denial so that some other insurance in place will consider paying a claim. In sum, both doctors who accept assignment and who do not accept assignment, file Medicare claims directly. You do not.

> *Doctors who **don't** accept Medicare assignment can charge more than doctors who **do**, and the Medicare payment goes to the patient, not the provider.*

Using the example above of the $100.00 Medicare approved charge, the doctor who does not accept assignment can get up to $115.00 for the service whereas the doctor who accepts assignment only receives $100.00. In both cases, Medicare only pays $80.00. If you have a Plan F Supplement, the richest Supplement which pays 100% after Medicare pays, then in this example, the Supplement will pay $35.00 to you for the doctor who does not accept assignment. If you have a private Supplement or retiree medical Plan that pays some portion after the $80.00 but less than $35.00, then you owe that balance to the doctor after the Plan pays. The doctor is due the full $115.00.

WAITING LISTS OR NOT ACCEPTING NEW MEDICARE PATIENTS

When you are told by a doctor's office that they are not accepting new Medicare patients or have a waiting list for new Medicare patients then you know that the office either accepts assignment or doesn't accept assignment. These offices have decided that Medicare payment rates are so low that they must limit the number of Medicare patients in the practice.

MEDICARE ADVANTAGE PLANS AND DOCTORS WHO ACCEPT OR DON'T ACCEPT ASSIGNMENT

Whether a doctor accepts Medicare assignment or not isn't relevant to a Medicare Advantage Plan. Advantage Plans have a network of doctors and you need to know which are in the network and if you want to see a doctor who is not in the network, whether you have out-of-network benefits. If you have out-of-network benefits, you'll typically pay a higher co-pay. When you're traveling outside of your local area, only urgent and emergent care would be covered with a Medicare Advantage Plan. In that case you would want to make sure you see a doctor who hasn't opted out of the Medicare Program altogether or you will have to pay cash.

DOCTORS WHO'VE OPTED OUT OF MEDICARE

An increasingly vexing issue concerns doctors who have chosen to have no relationship with Medicare. These doctors can charge you whatever they choose since they have no obligation to honor Medicare's approved charges. Doctors who opt out of Medicare tend to be internists or medical specialists of some sort, behavioral health providers, and, increasingly, gynecologists.

PRIVATE CONTRACT

That a doctor has opted out of Medicare should never come as a surprise. They are required to execute a so-called "private contract" with you which is a two or three page document which states that the doctor has no relationship with the Medicare program and you have agreed to pay cash. Medicare can't pay for services provided to a doctor who has no relationship with the Medicare program. However, if that doctor admits you to a hospital for a medically necessary admission, then Medicare does cover the other services that Medicare Parts A and B would have covered anyway. Only the fees associated with the physician(s) who has opted out will not be paid.

Doctors who have opted out of Medicare tend to be located in higher cost, affluent areas. They are doctors who have an established practice who believe most of their patients will stay with them even if those patients have to pay cash. Although we are seeing more gynecologists opt out of Medicare, we have only dealt with a handful of other types of surgeons who have opted out. Again, opting out of Medicare is typically more of an issue for the primary specialties, internists or medical subspecialists, psychiatrists, and other behavioral health providers.

If you have a Medicare Supplement, it does not pay for services associated with a doctor who has opted out of Medicare. Retiree medical secondary to Medicare often will pay a small amount of a medical bill from a doctor who has opted out of Medicare because the claim is typically processed as though the doctor participated with Medicare. These claims are almost always a headache because they need to be either sent in with a copy of the private contract or with a Medicare denial.

> *Doctors who have opted out of Medicare are required to execute a private contract with you, acknowledging that you understand you will pay cash for their services. Medicare will not pay any such claims.*

CONCIERGE MEDICINE

Doctors who've opted out of Medicare are often confused with "concierge" doctors but "concierge" doctors may or may not have opted out of Medicare. Concierge typically refers to a physician who is offering services beyond those covered by Medicare, like 24/7 access, email access and home visits, for an additional fee. In our experience, these fees range from a low of $1,500.00–$2,000.00 per year to about $15,000.00 although there are some services that charge more. The important issue is you should know what relationship your doctor has to the Medicare program so that you're not surprised.

Doctors not taking new Medicare patients, those maintaining a waiting list for those on Medicare, doctors opting out of Medicare altogether, and high fees for concierge services represent very frightening trends for all of us. To some extent we're paying the price for the way Medicare has cut physician payment rates over the years. This has been particularly difficult for primary care physicians whose charges are already low relative to specialists and whose practices tend to have a larger proportion of older, sicker patients with more intensive needs. **If you are on Medicare and your doctor is approaching retirement, you should think strategically about who your next doctor will be.**

Medicare Coordination of Benefits Issues

The term "coordination of benefits" refers to which source of coverage pays first. The most frequent problem we see with Medicare Coordination of Benefit issues relates to small groups of fewer than 20 employees. According to the rules of insurance and consistent with almost all insurance company approaches, if you have group coverage through your or a spouse's active employment through a group of under 20 employees, Medicare pays first and you should usually be on Medicare Parts A and B but not Part D. Medicare will be primary for medical services, the group Plan will be secondary and the group's drug Plan will provide drug coverage. There are some exceptions with insurance companies offering products that do not require Part B enrollment. Always verify that information in writing.

Sometimes Medicare has incorrect information on which source of coverage should be primary. We recently dealt with a situation where Medicare had recorded in its COB system a retired 96-year-old and his 94-year-old wife residing in a nursing home as having active group coverage as primary. The group could only have been primary if this couple had been actively employed. As you can imagine, their claims were a mess. Register on mymedicare.gov to see what information Medicare has on file. If it is not correct, you need to call the Medicare Coordination of Benefits (COB) Department so that your correct information is on file. You can do this by calling the Medicare Coordination of Benefits Department at 800-999-1118.

> *If your Medicare claims are not being processed properly, check your coverage information on mymedicare.gov then call the Medicare Coordination of Benefit (COB) Contractor to update it if needed.*

MEDICARE AND SMALL GROUP COB PROBLEMS

One new client came to us years ago. He and his wife owned a business together and they were each subscribers on this small group Plan. His broker had incorrectly advised him that he did not need to sign up for Medicare when he turned 65 because his group would continue to cover him. The broker was correct that this gentleman and his wife could keep the small group coverage but their insurance company actually required them to enroll in Medicare Parts A and B which would be primary. One blessing was that our client ignored the broker and did sign up for both Medicare Parts A and B. However, claims for medical services provided to this couple continued to be processed through the group coverage as primary.

Two years later, the gentleman's insurance carrier demanded repayment of all the claims they had paid as primary because his contract indicated Medicare should have been primary. They wanted almost $20,000.00 back. It wasn't an easy matter to deal with. Doctors' offices and other providers had to resubmit claims to Medicare as primary. Some of the claims were too old for Medicare to pay. After that, the responsibility of the small group Plan paying as secondary had to be determined. Many providers had been overpaid and owed a refund because they had originally been paid by the group Plan as primary and then subsequently paid by Medicare as primary. Yes, it was a mess. It cost this gentleman a good deal of money for our services to straighten this out.

Of course, it could have been worse. It was better that the client had enrolled in Medicare Part B even though his broker had misinformed him that he didn't need to. At least he had the Medicare as primary for most of the claims and didn't miss his Initial Enrollment Period.

Remember that verbal assurance from a broker is typically not going to absolve you from responsibility for a coordination of benefits problem even if you receive poor advice.

MEDICARE AND ACTIVE GROUP

We are seeing individuals who have excellent group coverage through their companies or small businesses getting poor advice about what they should be enrolled in. Sometimes that advice is coming from their companies, their brokers and sometimes they're just confused. Opting out of Medicare Part B is a very serious decision because Special Enrollment Period rules must be followed precisely. However, if your group coverage is so good that it's very unlikely you would use Part B, many higher income individuals and couples would decide to postpone enrollment in Part B because they don't want to pay for it until they need it.

We worked with an executive who was over 65 and employed by a large pharmaceutical and medical supply company which provided very good medical benefits. He was advised by his human resources department that he and his wife should enroll in Medicare Parts A and B. They were at the highest level of income-indexed Part B premiums so were paying between $600.00 and $700.00 per month for the two of them for several years because their large group was primary and their coverage so good. According to the client, he had paid about $15,000.00 for Part B for his wife and himself over several years and had never used it.

This gentleman contacted us because he wanted to know if he could drop the Part B.

We advised the couple that since they were both covered on a large group Plan through his active employment they didn't need to be on Part B and would have a Special Enrollment Period on his retirement. We would advise almost anyone in this situation to keep their premium-free Medicare Part A as secondary to the group which he and his wife did. We also advised him about how punitive the Part B rules are so he could plan his retirement to ensure no gap in coverage—not a single day—and enroll in Part B to coincide with his retirement.

STAYING ON PART B WITH LARGE GROUP COVERAGE

Some people are understandably anxious when they learn about the premium penalties associated with missing a Medicare Special Enrollment Period. As a result, some will choose to remain enrolled in Medicare Part B even if they have good group coverage and are unlikely to use their Part B coverage which would be secondary to the group. The important issue is to make an informed decision. Whether or not to maintain Part B coverage as secondary is a personal choice.

We worked with another gentleman who enrolled in Medicare Parts A, B and D who also had excellent active group coverage. In fact, he was the owner of his company of close to 100 employees. His insurance broker was very knowledgeable about the group health benefits but didn't understand Medicare. We advised the owner of his right to opt out of Medicare Parts B and D but to keep his premium-free Part A and that he needed to plan for coverage without a gap and without premium penalties upon retirement.

Every person who has active group coverage through a group of 20 or more employees needs to realize the group coverage is primary and enrolling in Medicare Part B is optional. Whether or not to enroll depends on a variety of factors and personal preferences. Our plea is to do your homework and maintain a personal Coverage Plan.

Ignorance Is Not Bliss

I'm partial to facts over "clues" about healthcare coverage. We have dealt with people who didn't know whether they were enrolled in Medicare or which parts of Medicare, had signed on to a Medicare Advantage Plan without knowing they had, didn't know anything about their secondary coverage, didn't know if they had long term care coverage, etc., etc.

At a certain age it's important that both spouses and someone else—a younger relative or for our clients, a firm like ours, have information. We have dealt with adult daughters of our clients who have flown into town due to a parent's illness and had no idea what their parent's coverage was, who their doctors were, or what pharmacy they used.

Every older individual or couple should have both a paper file and an electronic file that at a minimum includes:
* Copies of insurance cards
* Physician information
* Hospital and pharmacy preferences
* Living will and healthcare proxy documents

Sudden illness can strike at any time.
Give another responsible adult your
Medicare, other coverage information
and list of doctors and prescription drugs.

Learning about healthcare coverage may not be fun but a lot of financial matters aren't fun. The stakes are just too high for anyone to be uninformed.

MEDICARE SUMMARY

Medicare is under enormous financial strain. Public policy approaches to Medicare are inherently contradictory because Medicare is an enormously cherished benefit to so many people on Medicare and yet most informed sources acknowledge the current system is unsustainable due to a variety of factors including the population bulge of baby-boomers being on Medicare rather than paying to support Medicare.

As a result, it's more important than ever to understand when you need to enroll in Medicare. It should only be during the Initial Enrollment Period or a Special Enrollment Period—not the General Enrollment Period. Timely enrollment is critical in order to maintain proper coverage without a gap and to avoid Part B or Part D premium penalties.

You also need to understand the various parts of Medicare and your options with respect to retiree medical, Medicare Supplements, Medicare Advantage Plans and Part D Prescription Drug Plans. And the environment is changing, and will continue to change, so work done this year can't be relied on several years from now.

AFTERWORD

D ear reader, if you're still with me, I commend you. This is not easy material and even as I complete this work I am rather conflicted about it. I started graduate school in public health at Yale in 1976 and the healthcare field has been described as "in crisis" since my first day in the program. In 1977, I worked on a Yale Study Group Report which began:

> *The past decade has seen an unprecedented escalation of healthcare costs in the United States. All of the participants in the healthcare system—consumers, providers, third party insurers, and the government—are interested in fashioning more rational health delivery mechanisms in the hopes of containing that escalation.*[1]

Fast forward from 1977; not much has changed since 1977—except everything costs much, much more.

On the one hand, our work at Healthcare Navigation is immensely satisfying. We help people. On the other hand, I have spent my entire adult career in healthcare and have witnessed it becoming increasingly dysfunctional in spite of all the good intentions and good work of so many people. Numerous times clients have told me that we saved their lives. Think about

---

[1] Yale University Study Group headed by Professor John D. Thompson
submitted to Subcommittee on Oversight and Investigation,
U.S. House of Representatives, May 1977

that! Saving a life should be limited exclusively to doctors, other clinicians or emergency personnel. It is a great American tragedy that our healthcare system itself generates such stress.

This is not a book about policy. If anything, my concern about the current healthcare debate is so many believing that ACA, or any legislation for that matter, could be a panacea for all that is wrong with healthcare in the United States. We need more than what any legislation can do—greater emphasis on prevention, an anti-obesity movement akin to the anti-smoking movement, personal responsibility for healthy behaviors, improved methods of coordinating medical services, a culture of mindfulness that precious medical resources are finite, and new ways of delivering high quality primary care services and managing chronic disease, to name but a few critical initiatives.

As far as policy is concerned, in the U.S. we've managed to limp along with our patchwork approach for decades and given the political polarization in our country about how best to move forward, we may continue on this dysfunctional course for some time. It is my great hope that with the information in this book you have become better educated and informed, that you have a greater understanding that healthcare coverage issues are complex and ever-changing, that you are more passionate about building a saner future for our children and their children, and that you are in a better position to protect all those you love.

Please share this book with anyone this information might help. Thank you.

APPENDIX

MORE INFORMATION ON COVERAGE OPTIONS

What is COBRA? As discussed previously, COBRA is a temporary extension of group coverage; premiums are paid by individuals. COBRA is the acronym for Consolidated Omnibus Budget Reconciliation Act of 1985.

When should you consider COBRA? As a temporary bridge between jobs, a transition to age 65 and Medicare eligibility, when you have pre-existing condition in a state where individual insurance is medically underwritten or when it's a cheaper option than individual coverage in your state.

What is private, individual coverage? Healthcare coverage for an individual, couple or family purchased privately. In most states, individual coverage is "medically underwritten" meaning the application is accompanied by a health questionnaire and coverage can be denied.

In five states, New York, New Jersey, Maine, Massachusetts and, recently, Vermont, individual coverage is "guaranteed access" meaning you are entitled to the coverage as a state resident without respect to pre-existing conditions. In most guaranteed issue states, a pre-existing condition exclusion can be applied if you've had a gap in coverage of 63 days or more (HIPAA rule).

When should you consider private, individual coverage? When you will likely qualify, be accepted by the insurer and the insurance is a less expensive option than your alternatives. If you are planning to move in the near future you should know that private, individual coverage is often tied to your state of residence so in insurance terms, it is probably not "portable."

What is a State High Risk Pool? Thirty-four states have High Risk Pool Programs for individuals who have pre-existing conditions and won't be accepted for private, individual coverage which is medically underwritten. These programs vary widely. Some state programs are limited to those who are "HIPAA-eligible," (which is triggered by loss of group coverage). Some states require you to exhaust COBRA before applying for the High Risk Pool. Some programs require that you have a denial from a private insurance company within a certain timeframe before applying. Some will allow you to enroll if you want to give up individual coverage that is worse than the coverage the High Risk Pool Program offers; others will not. Some have a waiting list. You need to understand your state's requirements if state High Risk Pool insurance is a viable option for you.

When should you consider a State High Risk Pool? This is coverage of last resort. You usually enroll because you have no other options. In states where premiums are age-rated or based on age, High Risk Pool premiums can be quite expensive for older adults because premiums are based on an older and by definition, sicker, population. Insurance through a state High Risk Pool can be a much more affordable option for a younger adult.

What is the temporary federal Pre-existing Condition High Risk Pool? This is the temporary High Risk Pool Program established by the Affordable Care Act (ACA) legislation. The program should end in 2014 assuming ACA is implemented at which time all coverage would be issued without respect to pre-existing conditions. You have to have a pre-existing condition and have had no coverage for six months to qualify for this coverage in your state. Some states are running the program themselves; in other states the federal government is running the state program.

When should you consider the temporary federal Pre-existing Condition High Risk Pool? If you are not eligible for any other coverage, have a pre-existing condition, and have been without coverage for six months, this may be your best option for coverage. You should compare this option with the state High Risk Pool if your state has both but often being without coverage for six months would make you ineligible for the state program or a pre-existing condition exclusion period might apply. It depends on the state.

What is conversion coverage? This is an option for coverage in a handful of states that do not maintain High Risk Pools and are not like states where all people can get individual coverage because of state residency. Conversion coverage is an option for those exhausting their COBRA. State programs differ. The carrier providing your coverage may have to extend conversion coverage, all major insurers in the state may have to provide conversion coverage, and in a couple of states the Blue Cross and Blue Shield Plan provides the conversion coverage.

On occasion but rarely, we will find someone who still has a conversion option unrelated to the above described HIPAA-mandated option. When such an option has been available, it has been an extremely expensive option. Conversion used to be common but in the current era where no one wants to assume risk, it's fairly rare in the private insurance marketplace.

When should you consider conversion coverage? Like state High Risk Pool Programs, this is usually coverage of last resort and typically you would apply only if you had no other options.

What is sole proprietor coverage? A type of group healthcare coverage available in many states to those who are self-employed and considered "a group of one." The advantage of sole proprietor coverage is that, like group coverage it is not medically underwritten, so if you are eligible, it is provided without respect to pre-existing conditions. Unlike group coverage, there may be no COBRA right for the sole proprietor or dependents.

When should you consider sole proprietor coverage? Sole proprietor coverage can be an excellent option depending on the state, particularly if there's a family member with a pre-existing condition. A sole proprietor may have a pre-existing condition which makes him or her unattractive as an applicant for private, individual coverage even if that person is still totally productive and functioning. If it's an option, coverage through a group of two, i.e. two owners or an owner and employee, is preferable to sole proprietor coverage if there are dependents. Recall the problem Luci Watson had with no COBRA available after her husband's death. Also, Medicare does not recognize sole proprietor coverage as group coverage so there is no Special Enrollment Period for those on this type of coverage.

What is Association coverage? Healthcare coverage for an individual but provided through a group that an individual belongs to like the Freelancers Union, the Authors Guild, The American College of Surgeons or the American Bar Association, for example. It is always advisable to know if an Association Plan falls under a state's regulatory authority with appeal rights in case of dispute. There are some good options through an Association Plan but we have seen some very bad options as well.

When should you consider Association coverage? Depending on your state of residence and the product, Association coverage can be an excellent option if you are eligible. However, some Association coverage can be outrageously expensive and still not provide very good protection. A client came to us recently with Association coverage. Premiums were $20,000.00 per year for coverage that did not include a prescription drug benefit. He was eligible to enroll in the State High Risk Pool Plan which was expensive but far less than $20,000.00 per year and offered much more comprehensive coverage.

What is small group coverage? Small group coverage is insurance provided through a small business. The most important thing to know about small group coverage is that it can generally be a group as small as two people, two owners, an owner and an employee working the required hours, sometimes even just one covered person with the other owner or employee eligible but "waiving" the coverage because that person has coverage through another source.

When should you consider small group coverage? Small group coverage can be an excellent option and should always be considered if it's an option for you especially if it's your business. The rates for a very small group can be higher than a larger group but it's based on eligibility for coverage rather than on health status. We have worked with families who legitimately brought family members into ownership positions in a family business motivated by the ability to provide healthcare coverage. If you own a small business and can afford to pay for healthcare coverage through it, you have more control than many in today's healthcare environment.

What is large group coverage? Large group insurance is typically offered by employers of 50 or more even though those are fairly small businesses. Large group coverage can be a fully insured product (see Concepts and Terms in Appendix) regulated by the state the company is in or a self-insured Plan regulated by the federal government and referred to as health and welfare programs. Large group includes union Plans, too.

When should you consider large group coverage? You almost always want to take advantage of large group coverage when you, a spouse, or children are eligible for it because in general, it is comprehensive coverage and often the employer is subsidizing the coverage not only for the worker but also dependents. We have seen many clients maintain individual coverage in addition to their group coverage because they are anxious about losing their group coverage. That's a personal decision but often unnecessary because of the protections that COBRA and HIPAA provide.

What is Medicare? Medicare is coverage through the federal government. Most people are eligible at age 65 because they paid into Social Security as workers or were married the required period to someone who paid into Social Security long enough. You can also get Medicare through the

Railroad Retirement Board (RRB) if your Medicare payroll taxes went to the RRB.

When should you consider Medicare? With few exceptions, Medicare should be your primary coverage at age 65 unless you or your spouse work for a company of 20 or more people that offers group coverage.

How do you learn about healthcare coverage options?
COBRA: Employers are obligated to inform you of your COBRA rights when leaving a job or position. In the case of divorce, you are obligated to inform the employer of this "qualifying event" since only a spouse rather than a divorced spouse is eligible for coverage on the Plan.

Private, health coverage in my state: A local broker, the website of an insurance company, or ehealthinsurance are common ways to learn about individual insurance where you live.

In New York, New Jersey, Maine, Massachusetts, and Vermont, go to the State Insurance Department website. In Massachusetts, also go to www.mahealthconnector.org and insurance company websites.

High Risk Pool Program in my state: These High Risk Pool Programs have different names but there is usually information on your State Insurance Department website that will lead you to the High Risk Pool Program website for information. You can also check www.statehealthfacts.org.

Temporary federal Pre-Existing Condition High Risk Pool: Your State Insurance Department website will usually lead you to the state Program website or just go to a search engine and enter your state and "Pre-existing Insurance Plan."

Conversion coverage: There should be information on your State Insurance Department website or a link or go to a search engine and enter your state and "Conversion coverage" or go to www.statehealthfacts.org and search under your state.

Sole proprietor coverage: A reputable insurance broker is an excellent source of information about sole proprietor coverage. The state Insurance Department website also may be a good source of information. If you have difficulty you can always call your Insurance Department and ask for a health and life examiner and ask them the question and where to go for information.

Association coverage: Learning about good Association coverage options is more of a challenge. You should think of groups you belong to and inquire about whether obtaining health insurance through them is an option. You have to be very careful with Association coverage. Compare it side-by-side with your other options. We have seen excellent Association coverage options and outrageous options—the awful combination of poor coverage and high premiums.

Small group coverage: You can learn about small group coverage through private insurance brokers, insurance company representatives and websites, local business and industry associations, and sites like ehealthinsurance.com.

Large group coverage: You receive information from the group—the employer or union. Because the client is the group and not the individual, often you'll receive a rather skeletal summary of choices if you're lucky enough to have choices, during open enrollment which is often an on-line process with larger companies. To understand more about your current large group coverage, register on your insurance company website(s) to view the benefit and claim information available there.

How to learn about Medicare: Read the Medicare Traps and Gaps portion of this book, consult the *Medicare and You* book published every year by CMS (Center for Medicare and Medicaid Services), go to www.medicare.gov, call 1-800-MEDICARE, or go to www.aoa.gov (Administration on Aging).

What other types of health insurance coverage are there?
There's a staggering array of types of coverage available in the private market and through various government sources. There are also products that are simply discounts from a network of providers. These often masquerade as insurance. Be careful. If you get a fax at the office touting some program or Plan that's too good to be true, it probably is too good to be true. Call your state Insurance Department to find out if it's legitimate.

What follows is not an all-inclusive list by any means but identifies other common sources of coverage.

Mini-med Plans: These are limited benefit Plans typically provided by employers of lower income earners like restaurant chain employees. The coverage is typically not considered comprehensive enough to be "creditable" largely due to the limited benefits. The ACA seeks to eliminate these types of Plans although many have been granted grandfathered status for now. Sometimes an individual can purchase what's called a Limited Benefit Plan as well. Such Plans are better than having no coverage at all but having more comprehensive coverage is preferable.

Short-term insurance: Insurance which can be purchased on a month-to-month basis as a bridge to other coverage. This type of coverage excludes pre-existing conditions and is not available in all states.

Student health Plans: Coverage provided through a school to its students. The protection provided by Student Health Plans varies widely. Some Plans are very limited and would never be a good protection against serious illness. Student Health Plans should always be evaluated to understand how comprehensive the coverage is. If the Plan is limited, it may not be considered creditable which can leave you at risk for a new Plan imposing pre-existing condition exclusions.

Retiree coverage: Coverage provided through a former employer or union to those who have worked long enough to be eligible for the coverage. The value of retiree coverage varies widely. Sometimes it is subsidized and an extremely important benefit; at other times the retiree has better options depending on the circumstance. If the retiree opts out of retiree coverage, the retiree usually cannot get back on the Plan.

Travel coverage: Coverage which helps pay for medical expenses and/or medical evacuation when you are outside of your home country.

TYPES OF COVERAGE—GOVERNMENT SPONSORED

There are many types of government sponsored insurance. This is a brief list of major programs.

Medicare: A federal program providing hospital, medical and drug benefits to those 65 and over who have earned Medicare. Individuals who are totally disabled or have end-stage renal disease or Amyotrophic Lateral Sclerosis (ALS or Lou Gehrig's disease), may also be eligible for Medicare.

Medicaid: A federal program for indigent and low income Americans to provide hospital, medical and drug benefits. The majority of those on Medicaid are poorer Americans who rely on Medicaid for medical services and those who live permanently in a nursing home and have exhausted their assets.

State Children's Health Insurance Program (SCHIP): A program which provides federal funds to the states to help cover uninsured children. Children who may not qualify for Medicaid may qualify for SCHIP.

TRICARE: Retiree coverage for career military and their spouses.

Veterans Affairs coverage: Healthcare coverage provided to those who served in the military.

LAWS AND TERMS YOU SHOULD KNOW

Federal Laws

COBRA: The Consolidated Omnibus Budget Reconciliation Act of 1985, a federal law, intended to help workers and their families maintain coverage when facing a loss of coverage due to various types of transitions like job loss, reduction in hours worked, changing jobs, death, divorce, aging off a parent's Plan, and other life events. Federal law applies to groups of 20 or more employees. Many states extend similar benefits to employees of smaller companies through state laws referred to as "mini-COBRA."

ERISA: Employee Retirement Income Security Act, a federal law, governs how larger self-insured employers manage their employee and retiree benefits, including so-called health and welfare Plans and pensions. Many people whose Plans are governed under ERISA don't realize they may not have the ability in a dispute to appeal to their local State Insurance Department.

HIPAA: The Health Insurance Portability and Accountability Act, a federal law, intended to protect workers and their families covered by group Plans by limiting pre-existing condition exclusions. This law also provides an individual the right to purchase coverage in a state when he/she has exhausted COBRA coverage.

PPACA: The Patient Protection and Affordable Care Act of 2010, federal legislation modeled on Massachusetts health reforms, intended to extend coverage to millions of additional Americans in 2014 through subsidies and by requiring almost all Americans to obtain coverage or pay a fine, referred to as the individual insurance mandate. Many states have sued the federal government over the mandate. The Supreme Court has agreed to consider the constitutionality of several provisions of ACA in 2012. This is a massive piece of legislation with provisions taking effect between 2010 and 2020. Under this legislation all states are to have "insurance exchanges" in place by 2014 where all individuals can buy coverage on a "guaranteed issue" basis.

Terms

Creditable coverage: Insurance which is considered comprehensive and thus maintained without a gap in coverage. It prevents a new group Plan from imposing pre-existing condition exclusions. Under HIPAA, Plans must provide a "Letter of Creditable Coverage" when group coverage is terminated.

Dependents: Members of one's family or domestic partners entitled to the benefits of the coverage in place. **An ex-spouse is NEVER an eligible dependent but typically has a right to continued coverage through COBRA.**

Eligibility: The term that defines who is legitimately entitled to the benefits of the coverage whether individual, group or retiree. With individual coverage, this term usually applies to the applicant and applicant's eligible dependents such as spouse and children. With individual coverage, state of residency is often an eligibility requirement. With group coverage, the employee or union member who works the required hours is eligible for coverage as are his/her spouse, children and, at times, domestic partner. Retiree medical coverage eligibility is typically based on length of service with a company or union and usually includes eligible spouses although not necessarily survivor benefits should the retiree predecease the spouse.

Enrollment: The process for getting an eligible person onto an insurance Plan.

Exclusion: Anything specifically excluded from coverage.

Fully insured healthcare coverage: Coverage where the insurer assumes the financial risk of the claims (as opposed to a self-insured product where a union or group may assume that risk). Individual and small group insurance products are typically fully insured, regulated by the State's Insurance Department and required to include state mandated benefits in their coverage. State mandated benefits, explained on the next page, result from a special interest group, sometimes a patient advocacy group and sometimes a group of providers or suppliers, lobbying for legislation passed in their state to require insurers to cover a benefit.

Guaranteed issue: Coverage one can apply for that is automatically issued if one is eligible for the coverage. This term describes individual coverage in those states that do not allow medical underwriting in the individual insurance marketplace like New York, New Jersey, Maine, Massachusetts and Vermont, state High Risk Pool Programs (insurance for people who can't qualify for individual insurance due to health), and some states conversion options under HIPAA. This term is used when discussing individual coverage because coverage through an employer or union is guaranteed if the employer offers coverage and the employee elects it and works the required hours to be eligible. A good clue that individual coverage is "guaranteed issue" in the application, which often requires proving residency in your state.

Mandates: Benefits mandated by a state often as a result of lobbying efforts either on the part of a patient group or provider group. Mental health benefits are a good example of a mandate. There are numerous state mental health benefit mandates and there is also a federal health parity law which requires that insurers cover behavioral health services like medical services.

Medical underwriting: Considering an applicant's health in the approval process for individual insurance. In most states, individual insurance is medically underwritten and the insurer has the right to deny applicants with pre-existing conditions. Under ACA, medical underwriting would be discontinued in 2014 and all coverage would be provided on a "guaranteed issue" basis.

Qualifying event: This term is used to describe a life transition that makes you eligible to enroll in coverage off-cycle from an Annual Enrollment Period because you are no longer eligible for your existing coverage. Qualifying events lead to enrollment rights for coverage or COBRA depending on the situation for both those who held the coverage as well as dependents. Qualifying events include turning 26, losing or quitting a job, divorce, a spouse's retirement, and death of a spouse. Birth, marriage and at times domestic partner status make us eligible for coverage but these are not considered qualifying events as such.

Rider: A provision attached to a policy. Sometimes it's an additional benefit but it can also be a description of an exclusion.

Self-insured: Coverage provided by an employer or union in which the company or firm assumes the financial risk of claims to a given level and retains an insurer to process claims rather than assume risk. Unlike fully insured coverage, self-insured Plans are regulated under federal law which enables them to bypass state insurance mandates for certain benefits, giving them more discretion to decide which benefits they will offer to covered individuals.

Subscriber: The person who is the primary applicant for individual coverage, the eligible employee or union member for group coverage, or eligible retiree for retiree medical group coverage.

Waiting period: Aptly named, a length of time before a benefit will be honored.

PCIP and MRMIP Monthly Premiums | Area 3

Use this chart to compare premiums based on your age and where you live.

Premiums for people who live in: Alameda, Contra Costa, Marin, San Francisco, San Mateo, and Santa Clara counties. Some health plans may not be available in your area – see notes below.

---

4. Contra Costa Health Plan is available only in **Contra Costa County.**

5. Kaiser Permanente Northern California serves all ZIP codes in **Alameda, Contra Costa, Marin, San Francisco,** and **San Mateo** counties and these ZIP codes in this county: **Santa Clara** 94022-24, 94035, 94039-43, 94085-89,

94301-06, 94309, 95002, 95008-09, 95011, 95013-15, 95020-21, 95026, 95030-33, 95035-38, 95042, 95044, 95046, 95050-56, 95070-71, 95101, 95103, 95106, 95108-13, 95115-36, 95138-41, 95148, 95150-61, 95164, 95170, 95172-73, 95190-94, and 95196.

Premiums effective through December 31, 2012

	PCIP	MRMIP								
		In MRMIP, you get your health care through a health plan. Premiums for the health plans are listed below.								
	Subscriber only	Subscriber only			Subscriber and 1 dependent			Subscriber and 2 or more dependents		
Age	PCIP	Anthem Blue Cross PPO	Contra Costa Health Plan[4]	Kaiser Permanente N. California[5]	Anthem Blue Cross PPO	Contra Costa Health Plan[4]	Kaiser Permanente N. California[5]	Anthem Blue Cross PPO	Contra Costa Health Plan[4]	Kaiser Permanente N. California[5]
0 – 14	$124.00	$396.00	$268.35	$281.50	$785.00	$662.17	$561.88	$1,235.00	$1,220.80	$974.04
15 – 18	$124.00	$518.00	$341.28	$354.06	$1,060.00	$662.17	$747.59	$1,745.00	$1,220.80	$1,224.26
19 – 29	$171.00	$518.00	$341.28	$354.06	$1,060.00	$662.17	$747.59	$1,745.00	$1,220.80	$1,224.26
30 – 34	$247.00	$715.00	$495.84	$418.36	$1,257.00	$878.70	$850.48	$2,073.00	$1,349.45	$1,481.46
35 – 39	$275.00	$815.00	$495.84	$449.24	$1,368.00	$878.70	$937.91	$2,250.00	$1,349.45	$1,481.46
40 – 44	$305.00	$859.00	$571.16	$504.10	$1,494.00	$1,085.82	$1,028.78	$2,311.00	$1,606.81	$1,503.75
45 – 49	$346.00	$912.00	$571.16	$553.86	$1,804.00	$1,085.82	$1,078.53	$2,584.00	$1,606.81	$1,503.75
50 – 54	$428.00	$1,168.00	$762.59	$639.58	$2,281.00	$1,487.56	$1,285.99	$2,987.00	$1,839.03	$1,663.21
55 – 59	$514.00	$1,404.00	$762.59	$732.16	$2,773.00	$1,487.56	$1,424.89	$3,439.00	$1,839.03	$1,663.21
60 – 64	$557.00	$1,771.00	$963.45	$811.03	$3,375.00	$1,920.65	$1,622.08	$4,065.00	$2,231.32	$1,879.28
65 – 69	$557.00	$1,984.00	$1,292.97	$1,354.51	$3,780.00	$2,520.04	$2,402.18	$4,553.00	$2,988.48	$3,121.43
70 – 74	$557.00	$2,090.00	$1,292.97	$1,429.93	$3,983.00	$2,520.04	$2,534.53	$4,797.00	$2,988.48	$3,299.80
> 74	$557.00	$2,214.00	$1,292.97	$1,517.08	$4,219.00	$2,520.04	$2,680.48	$5,082.00	$2,988.48	$3,490.98

10

State High Risk Pool Rates–California

HRA Rates

Health Reinsurance Association
Serving Connecticut since 1976

Home   About Us   Brochures   Rates   Links   FAQ

Individual

Conversion

Portability
   PPO
   SHCP

TAA

2011 HRA PLAN RATES
Monthly Premium Rates per Individual
PPO Portability Plan

Attained Age	Male	Female	Child(ren)
<30	$431.62	$840.01	$631.43
30-34	$522.16	$883.03	
35-39	$574.36	$869.66	
40-44	$689.21	$910.41	
45-49	$851.86	$991.29	
50-54	$1,122.54	$1,138.78	
55-59	$1,469.09	$1,330.48	
60-64	$1,874.74	$1,588.12	
65+ Medicare Primary	$1,293.57	$1,095.80	

Please note: When you or any covered family member has a birthday that moves you to the next age bracket, the rate will change the month after the birthday occurs.

How to figure out your cost of coverage

1. Go to the above rate chart and get a rate for your coverage based on you age and gender.
2. Get rates for other family members to be covered based on their ages and genders. (The rate shown for "child(ren)" is a flat rate for all your children, no matter how many are covered.)
3. Add together all the rates for your family members. This is your monthly cost of coverage.

Health Reinsurance Association (CT)

1 800 842 0004

http://www.hract.org/hra/Rates/2011/Portability/PorPPORates.htm

11/3/2011

State High Risk Pool Rates—Connecticut

ILLINOIS

COMPREHENSIVE

HEALTH

INSURANCE

PLAN

Premium Rate Tables and Instructions

Information and Premium Rates contained herein are subject to change without notice

A State Program for Eligible Illinois Residents who are Unable to Obtain Private Health Insurance Coverage. This Rate Table Includes Rates for Persons Who Select Either Standard Coverage or a High Deductible Health Plan Option.

Effective August 1, 2011

00116.0811 (Rev 10.11)

State High Risk Pool Rates–Illinois

AUGUST 2011 RATE AREA A - The City of Chicago, Cook County only.

MONTHLY PREMIUM RATE FOR HIPAA STANDARD AND HIGH DEDUCTIBLE HEALTH PLAN (PLANS 5 and 5-H)

For Quarterly Rates, multiply the monthly rates by three; for semiannual, multiply the monthly rates by six

Non-Tobacco User

Age	M Std $500	M $1,000	M $1,500	M $2,500	M $5,000	M HDHP $1,200	M $2,000	M $5,200	F Std $500	F $1,000	F $1,500	F $2,500	F $5,000	F HDHP $1,200	F $2,000	F $5,200
Under 20	243	212	191	159	124	208	142	105	253	226	203	170	134	219	150	112
20-29	292	253	229	191	151	242	167	124	423	375	333	278	221	345	236	181
30-34	338	289	263	219	174	271	188	141	488	418	377	318	252	392	269	207
35	368	318	287	241	191	295	203	156	511	437	397	331	263	411	285	219
36	379	328	297	247	197	304	210	159	518	445	403	337	268	421	290	224
37	390	338	305	255	202	312	218	165	527	453	410	342	272	432	298	229
38	408	351	320	267	212	327	227	173	540	464	421	353	280	442	306	235
39	425	367	332	278	220	339	236	181	554	477	431	362	287	454	315	243
40	446	385	349	294	233	351	247	190	571	490	443	373	296	466	323	249
41	464	401	363	305	242	366	258	198	582	502	454	381	304	477	331	255
42	484	417	377	318	252	382	267	207	596	512	464	389	310	487	339	262
43	509	438	397	333	266	401	283	219	610	527	477	400	319	502	349	270
44	532	459	417	350	278	421	297	229	628	540	489	411	328	516	359	278
45	564	486	441	371	294	444	314	243	647	558	506	424	337	531	371	285
46	589	509	461	388	308	464	328	258	663	572	519	434	345	542	380	290
47	615	530	480	406	322	487	344	269	679	586	531	445	354	558	391	298
48	644	557	504	424	338	513	362	283	697	602	546	458	364	575	401	308
49	676	583	529	444	354	538	380	297	718	619	562	471	374	591	414	318
50	715	617	559	470	374	570	402	315	740	640	581	487	388	609	427	328
51	746	644	583	490	390	594	421	329	762	659	597	501	397	626	440	338
52	775	670	608	510	406	623	440	344	781	676	614	514	408	643	452	348
53	818	706	640	538	427	655	463	362	798	690	627	527	418	657	462	356
54	862	745	673	565	450	693	489	380	818	707	643	540	428	676	475	366
55	915	791	716	602	478	738	520	405	842	729	661	557	441	695	492	379
56	961	829	750	631	501	775	547	425	862	746	677	570	451	713	506	390
57	1005	868	785	659	523	815	574	445	883	764	694	582	462	736	520	401
58	1051	909	820	688	547	852	599	463	907	784	712	598	473	755	532	411
59	1099	949	859	719	571	893	628	486	932	807	732	615	487	779	549	424
60	1158	1001	904	757	602	941	662	512	964	834	756	636	503	806	571	440
61	1205	1041	941	789	626	973	687	530	988	854	775	651	515	824	583	450
62	1250	1080	976	818	650	1006	707	548	1009	873	791	666	527	840	593	458
63	1314	1136	1026	860	683	1049	739	574	1049	907	823	690	548	866	614	473
64	1377	1191	1075	902	715	1090	770	598	1085	938	851	715	566	890	631	486
*65-69	1495	1292	1164	977	774	1182	835	647	1148	993	902	757	600	942	668	514
*70-74	1659	1433	1293	1085	860	1312	927	719	1253	1085	982	825	655	1027	729	563
*75+	1853	1602	1445	1214	961	1468	1037	803	1357	1175	1066	894	711	1113	790	609

Tobacco User

Age	M Std $500	M $1,000	M $1,500	M $2,500	M $5,000	M HDHP $1,200	M $2,000	M $5,200	F Std $500	F $1,000	F $1,500	F $2,500	F $5,000	F HDHP $1,200	F $2,000	F $5,200
Under 20	306	268	241	201	157	262	180	132	319	285	257	214	170	276	190	141
20-29	367	319	289	241	191	305	210	157	532	472	420	350	279	434	297	228
30-34	426	365	332	276	219	341	236	179	615	527	476	400	318	494	339	261
35	464	400	362	303	241	372	257	197	644	551	499	417	332	519	359	276
36	477	412	374	312	247	383	264	201	652	560	509	424	338	531	366	281
37	492	426	384	322	255	393	275	208	663	571	516	432	344	544	376	289
38	514	443	403	336	268	411	286	218	680	585	531	444	353	557	385	296
39	536	463	418	350	278	427	297	228	697	601	542	455	362	573	398	306
40	563	486	440	371	294	443	312	240	719	618	558	470	373	586	407	313
41	585	505	457	384	305	461	324	250	733	632	573	480	383	601	417	322
42	609	525	476	400	318	481	336	261	750	645	585	489	390	614	427	330
43	641	553	499	420	334	505	356	276	768	663	601	504	401	632	440	340
44	670	579	525	442	350	531	374	289	792	680	617	519	412	651	453	350
45	711	612	555	467	371	559	396	306	816	703	637	534	424	669	467	359
46	741	641	581	488	389	585	412	324	836	721	653	547	434	684	478	366
47	774	668	606	511	406	614	433	339	855	739	669	560	445	703	493	376
48	811	702	635	534	426	646	455	356	878	759	688	576	459	724	505	389
49	851	735	667	559	445	678	478	374	904	780	707	593	471	745	521	400
50	902	777	705	592	471	718	507	398	932	806	732	614	488	767	538	412
51	940	811	735	618	492	749	531	415	959	831	751	631	499	789	554	426
52	976	844	766	642	511	784	554	433	984	851	773	647	514	810	570	438
53	1031	890	806	678	538	826	584	455	1006	870	790	663	527	827	582	449
54	1086	938	849	712	566	872	617	478	1031	892	810	680	540	851	598	461
55	1154	997	903	759	602	930	655	510	1061	919	833	702	555	876	619	477
56	1210	1045	946	794	631	976	689	536	1086	940	853	718	568	898	637	492
57	1266	1094	990	831	659	1026	723	560	1112	963	875	733	582	927	655	505
58	1324	1145	1034	867	689	1074	755	584	1144	988	897	754	597	951	670	519
59	1385	1196	1083	905	719	1124	792	612	1175	1017	922	774	614	981	692	534
60	1460	1261	1139	954	759	1187	834	645	1215	1051	953	801	634	1015	719	554
61	1518	1311	1187	993	789	1226	866	668	1244	1077	976	820	650	1038	735	566
62	1575	1362	1231	1031	819	1267	892	690	1271	1101	997	838	663	1058	748	576
63	1655	1431	1293	1084	860	1321	931	723	1321	1144	1036	870	690	1090	773	597
64	1736	1501	1354	1136	902	1374	970	754	1367	1182	1072	902	713	1122	794	612
*65-69	1884	1627	1467	1232	975	1489	1052	816	1446	1252	1136	954	756	1188	842	647
*70-74	2091	1806	1628	1367	1084	1653	1167	905	1579	1367	1237	1040	826	1294	919	709
*75+	2335	2019	1822	1529	1210	1850	1307	1012	1710	1480	1342	1127	896	1402	996	767

* Rates for ages 65 and over apply only if the person is not Medicare eligible. Persons eligible for Medicare are not eligible for any CHIP plan once they reach Medicare age.

Rev 10.11

-4-

State High Risk Pool Rates–Illinois

TEXAS HEALTH INSURANCE POOL
REGULAR
Monthly Premium Rate Table
Effective Date 01/01/2012

NON-TOBACCO USER

	Plan I $1,000 Deductible		Plan II $2,500 Deductible		Plan III $5,000 Deductible		Plan IV $7,500 Deductible		Plan V (HSAQ) $3,000 Deductible	
Area 1										
Age	Male	Female	Male	Female	Male	Female	Male	Female	Male	Female
0-18	$373	$373	$273	$273	$216	$216	$162	$162	$273	$273
19-24	$406	$541	$293	$388	$230	$307	$174	$233	$293	$388
25-29	$419	$586	$296	$425	$239	$332	$180	$249	$296	$425
30-34	$476	$646	$343	$463	$273	$367	$205	$276	$343	$463
35-39	$542	$699	$387	$504	$307	$402	$233	$301	$387	$504
40-44	$627	$766	$449	$552	$356	$438	$266	$328	$449	$552
45-49	$726	$830	$524	$593	$416	$469	$311	$351	$524	$593
50-54	$860	$908	$615	$655	$495	$523	$371	$393	$615	$655
55-59	$1,086	$993	$783	$717	$620	$570	$466	$426	$783	$717
60-64	$1,243	$1,175	$895	$847	$710	$670	$535	$501	$895	$847
Area 2										
Age	Male	Female	Male	Female	Male	Female	Male	Female	Male	Female
0-18	$420	$420	$301	$301	$240	$240	$181	$181	$301	$301
19-24	$454	$609	$332	$444	$257	$347	$193	$260	$332	$444
25-29	$470	$656	$338	$473	$271	$378	$203	$283	$338	$473
30-34	$539	$727	$388	$517	$306	$417	$232	$313	$388	$517
35-39	$609	$789	$433	$569	$347	$453	$260	$341	$433	$569
40-44	$705	$861	$506	$621	$404	$495	$303	$371	$506	$621
45-49	$816	$933	$588	$667	$466	$531	$350	$398	$588	$667
50-54	$967	$1,024	$697	$739	$552	$584	$412	$439	$697	$739
55-59	$1,222	$1,116	$879	$803	$699	$640	$525	$481	$879	$803
60-64	$1,405	$1,326	$1,012	$954	$801	$758	$601	$570	$1,012	$954
Area 3										
Age	Male	Female	Male	Female	Male	Female	Male	Female	Male	Female
0-18	$440	$440	$316	$316	$249	$249	$187	$187	$316	$316
19-24	$474	$631	$347	$461	$271	$359	$203	$271	$347	$461
25-29	$495	$687	$351	$497	$284	$393	$213	$296	$351	$497
30-34	$560	$757	$404	$544	$320	$435	$239	$326	$404	$544
35-39	$633	$826	$461	$592	$360	$469	$272	$351	$461	$592
40-44	$738	$902	$529	$650	$420	$514	$315	$388	$529	$650
45-49	$852	$974	$618	$697	$487	$553	$366	$413	$618	$697
50-54	$1,014	$1,075	$726	$769	$578	$613	$434	$460	$726	$769
55-59	$1,285	$1,172	$919	$842	$731	$666	$549	$500	$919	$842
60-64	$1,464	$1,387	$1,057	$999	$839	$794	$628	$595	$1,057	$999

Non-Tobacco User, Page 1 of 2

R01012012

State High Risk Pool Rates–Texas

REGULAR
Monthly Premium Rate Table
Effective Date 01/01/2012

NON-TOBACCO USER									
	Plan I $1,000 Deductible		Plan II $2,500 Deductible		Plan III $5,000 Deductible		Plan IV $7,500 Deductible		Plan V (HSAQ) $3,000 Deductible	
Area 4									
Age	Male	Female	Male	Female	Male	Female	Male	Female	Male	Female
0-18	$468	$468	$335	$335	$268	$268	$201	$201	$335	$335
19-24	$509	$675	$369	$491	$290	$384	$217	$288	$369	$491
25-29	$528	$738	$377	$529	$299	$420	$224	$315	$377	$529
30-34	$598	$808	$430	$581	$339	$462	$254	$347	$430	$581
35-39	$674	$871	$489	$633	$380	$502	$286	$376	$489	$633
40-44	$785	$962	$567	$689	$444	$548	$334	$410	$567	$689
45-49	$908	$1,037	$655	$744	$519	$592	$391	$445	$655	$744
50-54	$1,077	$1,140	$778	$821	$617	$648	$463	$486	$778	$821
55-59	$1,363	$1,245	$979	$895	$780	$712	$585	$536	$979	$895
60-64	$1,559	$1,475	$1,122	$1,060	$889	$843	$669	$633	$1,122	$1,060
Area 5									
Age	Male	Female	Male	Female	Male	Female	Male	Female	Male	Female
0-18	$491	$491	$351	$351	$283	$283	$212	$212	$351	$351
19-24	$531	$705	$387	$511	$300	$403	$225	$302	$387	$511
25-29	$556	$774	$399	$556	$316	$442	$236	$332	$399	$556
30-34	$629	$848	$451	$608	$359	$485	$271	$364	$451	$608
35-39	$711	$918	$511	$665	$404	$525	$303	$394	$511	$665
40-44	$822	$1,008	$593	$723	$467	$577	$350	$433	$593	$723
45-49	$957	$1,085	$689	$782	$546	$620	$409	$466	$689	$782
50-54	$1,128	$1,194	$810	$860	$644	$680	$485	$511	$810	$860
55-59	$1,430	$1,312	$1,029	$940	$817	$749	$614	$562	$1,029	$940
60-64	$1,637	$1,553	$1,179	$1,116	$932	$886	$699	$667	$1,179	$1,116
Area 6									
Age	Male	Female	Male	Female	Male	Female	Male	Female	Male	Female
0-18	$530	$530	$380	$380	$300	$300	$225	$225	$380	$380
19-24	$575	$761	$416	$555	$327	$438	$246	$328	$416	$555
25-29	$597	$832	$429	$596	$339	$470	$254	$352	$429	$596
30-34	$675	$916	$489	$655	$388	$524	$291	$393	$489	$655
35-39	$766	$988	$555	$710	$438	$564	$328	$424	$555	$710
40-44	$887	$1,082	$636	$783	$507	$620	$380	$466	$636	$783
45-49	$1,026	$1,173	$744	$842	$584	$667	$439	$501	$744	$842
50-54	$1,218	$1,291	$877	$929	$699	$739	$525	$554	$877	$929
55-59	$1,547	$1,410	$1,111	$1,012	$881	$806	$665	$605	$1,111	$1,012
60-64	$1,767	$1,670	$1,275	$1,203	$1,012	$955	$760	$716	$1,275	$1,203

Non-Tobacco User, Page 2 of 2

R01012012

State High Risk Pool Rates–Texas

FORM DOES NOT REQUIRE CLEARANCE
OF OFFICE OF MANAGEMENT AND BUDGET

APPLICATION FOR ENROLLMENT IN MEDICARE
THE MEDICAL INSURANCE PROGRAM

(TID)   **SMI**

1. SOCIAL SECURITY CLAIM NUMBER

(CAN) ☐ ☐ ☐ — ☐ ☐ — ☐ ☐ ☐ ☐

2. FOR AGENCY USE ONLY

(BIC) ☐ ☐ ☐

3. DO YOU WISH TO ENROLL FOR MEDICAL INSURANCE UNDER MEDICARE?

(DEC)   YES ☐

4. CLAIMANT'S NAME

(CLN)

Last name   First name   Middle initial

5. PRINT SOCIAL SECURITY NUMBER HOLDER'S NAME IF DIFFERENT FROM YOURS

6. MAILING ADDRESS (NUMBER AND STREET, P.O. BOX, OR ROUTE)

IF THIS IS A CHANGE OF ADDRESS, CHECK HERE ☐

7. CITY, STATE, AND ZIP CODE

8. TELEPHONE NUMBER

9. WRITTEN SIGNATURE (DO NOT PRINT)

SIGN HERE ➡ _____

10. DATE SIGNED

(DOF) __ __ / __ __ / __ __
MONTH   DAY   YEAR

IF THIS APPLICATION HAS BEEN SIGNED BY MARK (X), A WITNESS WHO KNOWS THE APPLICANT MUST SUPPLY THE INFORMATION REQUESTED BELOW

11. SIGNATURE OF WITNESS

12. DATE SIGNED

13. ADDRESS OF WITNESS

14. REMARKS

(TOA)   1

TO: (Check one)

☐ (1) NEPSC	☐ (2) MATPSC	☐ (3) SEPSC	☐ (4) GLPSC	☐ (5) WNPSC	☐ (6) MAMPSC	☐ (7) ODO	☐ (8) DIO

FORM CMS-40B (1-90)   EF (10-2001)

Medicare Part B Special Enrollment Form CMS-40B
(Call Social Security to obtain original form)

REQUEST FOR EMPLOYMENT INFORMATION

From: Telephone No.

Social Security Administration

Employer's Name and Address   Date:

                                                         Employee's Name:

                                                         Employee's Social Security Number:

                                                         Claimant's Name:

                                                         Claim Number:

Dear Sir/Madam:

We need the following information regarding the above claimant. Please answer the questions below, sign and date this letter and return it in the enclosed envelope.

You may call_____ at the above telephone number if you have any questions.

                                                         Sincerely,

                                                         Office Manager

1. Is (or was) the claimant covered under an Employer Group Health Plan?

    Yes _____   No _____

2. If yes, give the original date the coverage began. _____
                                                       (mm/yyyy)

3. Has the coverage ended?   Yes _____   No _____

4. If yes, give the date the coverage ended. _____
                                               (mm/yyyy)

5. When did the employee work for your company?

    From _____   To _____   Still Employed _____
         (mm/dd/yyyy)   (mm/dd/yyyy)

Signature and Title of Company Official   Date   Telephone Number

According to the Paperwork Reduction Act of 1995, no persons are required to respond to a collection of information unless it displays a valid OMB control number. The valid OMB control number for this information is 0938-0787. The time required to complete this information collection is estimated to average 15 minutes per response, including the time to review instructions, search existing data resources, gather the data needed, and complete and review the information collection. If you have any comments concerning the accuracy of the time estimate(s) or suggestions for improving this form, please write to: CMS, 7500 Security Boulevard, N2-14-26, Baltimore, Maryland 21244-1850.

FORM CMS-L564 (4-2000)

Medicare Part B Special Enrollment Form CMS-L564
(Call Social Security to obtain original form)

Medicare Income-Related Monthly Adjustment Amount - Life-Changing Event

If you had a major life-changing event and your income has gone down, you may use this form to request a reduction in your income-related monthly adjustment amount. See page 5 for detailed information and line-by-line instructions. If you prefer to schedule an interview with your local Social Security office, call 1-800-772-1213 (TTY 1-800-325-0778).

Name	Social Security Number

You may use this form if you received a notice that your monthly Medicare Part B (medical insurance) or prescription drug coverage premiums include an income-related monthly adjustment amount (IRMAA) and you experienced a life-changing event that may reduce your IRMAA. To decide your IRMAA, we asked the Internal Revenue Service (IRS) about your adjusted gross income plus certain tax-exempt income which we call "modified adjusted gross income" or MAGI from the Federal income tax return you filed for tax year 2010. If that was not available, we asked for your tax return information for 2009. We took this information and used the table below to decide your income-related monthly adjustment amount.

The table below shows the income-related monthly adjustment amounts for Medicare premiums based on your tax filing status and income. If your MAGI was lower than $85,000.01 (or lower than $170,000.01 if you filed your taxes with the filing status of married, filing jointly) in your most recent filed tax return, you do not have to pay any income-related monthly adjustment amount. If you do not have to pay an income-related monthly adjustment amount, you should not fill out this form even if you experienced a life-changing event.

If you filed your taxes as:	And your MAGI was:	Your Part B monthly adjustment is:	Your prescription drug coverage monthly adjustment is:
-Single, -Head of household, -Qualifying widow(er) with dependent child, or -Married filing separately (and you did not live with your spouse in tax year)*	$ 85,000.01 - $107,000.00 $107,000.01 - $160,000.00 $160,000.01 - $214,000.00 More than $214,000	$ 40.00 $ 99.90 $ 159.80 $ 219.80	$ 11.60 $ 29.90 $ 48.10 $ 66.40
-Married, filing jointly	$170,000.01 - $214,000.00 $214,000.01 - $320,000.00 $320,000.01 - $428,000.00 More than $428,000	$ 40.00 $ 99.90 $ 159.80 $ 219.80	$ 11.60 $ 29.90 $ 48.10 $ 66.40
-Married, filing separately (and you lived with your spouse during part of that tax year)*	$ 85,000.01 - $129,000.00 More than $129,000	$ 159.80 $ 219.80	$ 48.10 $ 66.40

* Let us know if your tax filing status for the tax year was Married, filing separately, but you lived apart from your spouse at all times during that tax year.

Form **SSA-44** (11-2011) Destroy Prior Editions   1

Medicare Income-Related Monthly Adjusted Amount—
Life Changing Event, SSA-44

STEP 1: Type of Life-Changing Event

Check **ONE** life-changing event and fill in the date that the event occurred (mm/dd/yyyy). If you had more than one life-changing event, please call Social Security at 1-800-772-1213 (TTY 1-800-325-0778).

☐ Marriage   ☐ Work Reduction

☐ Divorce/Annulment   ☐ Loss of Income-Producing Property

☐ Death of Your Spouse   ☐ Loss of Pension Income

☐ Work Stoppage   ☐ Employer Settlement Payment

Date of life-changing event: _____

mm/dd/yyyy

STEP 2: Reduction in Income

Fill in the tax year in which your income was reduced by the life-changing event (see instructions on page 6), the amount of your adjusted gross income (AGI, as used on line 37 of IRS form 1040) and tax-exempt interest income (as used on line 8b of IRS form 1040), and your tax filing status.

Tax Year	Adjusted Gross Income	Tax-Exempt Interest
2 0 _ _	$ _ _ _ _ _ . _ _	$ _ _ _ _ _ . _ _

Tax Filing Status for this Tax Year (choose **ONE**):

☐ Single   ☐ Head of Household   ☐ Qualifying Widow(er) with Dependent Child

☐ Married, Filing Jointly   ☐ Married, Filing Separately

STEP 3: Modified Adjusted Gross Income

Will your modified adjusted gross income be lower next year than the year in Step 2?

☐ No - Skip to STEP 4

☐ Yes - Complete the blocks below for next year

Tax Year	Estimated Adjusted Gross Income	Estimated Tax-Exempt Interest
2 0 _ _	$ _ _ _ _ _ . _ _	$ _ _ _ _ _ . _ _

Expected Tax Filing Status for this Tax Year (choose **ONE**):

☐ Single   ☐ Head of Household   ☐ Qualifying Widow(er) with Dependent Child

☐ Married, Filing Jointly   ☐ Married, Filing Separately

Form **SSA-44** (11-2011)   2

**Medicare Income-Related Monthly Adjusted Amount—
Life Changing Event, SSA-44**

STEP 4: Documentation

Provide evidence of your modified adjusted gross income (MAGI) and your life-changing event. You can either:

1. Attach the required evidence and we will mail your original documents or certified copies back to you;

OR

2. Show your original documents or certified copies of evidence of your life-changing event and modified adjusted gross income to an SSA employee.

Note: You must sign in Step 5 and attach all required evidence. Make sure that you provide your current address and a phone number so that we can contact you if we have any questions about your request.

STEP 5: Signature

PLEASE READ THE FOLLOWING INFORMATION CAREFULLY BEFORE SIGNING THIS FORM.

I understand that the Social Security Administration (SSA) will check my statements with records from the Internal Revenue Service to make sure the determination is correct.

I declare under penalty of perjury that I have examined the information on this form and it is true and correct to the best of my knowledge.

I understand that signing this form does not constitute a request for SSA to use more recent tax year information unless it is accompanied by:

- **Evidence that I have had the life-changing event indicated on this form;**
- **A copy of my Federal tax return; or**
- **Other evidence of the more recent tax year's modified adjusted gross income.**

Signature	Phone Number	
Mailing Address	**Apartment Number**	
City	**State**	**Zip Code**

Medicare Income-Related Monthly Adjusted Amount—
Life Changing Event, SSA-44

Benefit Chart of Medicare Supplement Plans Sold for Effective Dates on or After June 1, 2010

A	B	C	D	F/F*	G	K	L	M	N
Basic, including 100% Part B coinsurance	Basic, including 100% Part B coinsurance	Basic, including 100% Part B coinsurance	Basic, including 100% Part B coinsurance	Basic, including 100% Part B coinsurance	Basic, including 100% Part B coinsurance	Hospitalization and preventive care paid at 100%, other basic benefits paid at 50%	Hospitalization and preventive care paid at 100%, other basic benefits paid at 75%	Basic, including 100% Part B coinsurance	Basic, including 100% Part B coinsurance, except up to $20 copayment for office visit, and up to $50 copayment for emergency room
		Skilled Nursing Facility Coinsurance	Skilled Nursing Facility Coinsurance	Skilled Nursing Facility Coinsurance	Skilled Nursing Facility Coinsurance	50% Skilled Nursing Facility Coinsurance	75% Skilled Nursing Facility Coinsurance	Skilled Nursing Facility Coinsurance	Skilled Nursing Facility Coinsurance
	Part A Deductible	Part A Deductible	Part A Deductible	Part A Deductible	Part A Deductible	50% Part A Deductible	75% Part A Deductible	50% Part A Deductible	Part A Deductible
		Part B Deductible		Part B Deductible					
				Part B Excess (100%)	Part B Excess (100%)				
		Foreign Travel Emergency	Foreign Travel Emergency	Foreign Travel Emergency	Foreign Travel Emergency			Foreign Travel Emergency	Foreign Travel Emergency
						Out-of-pocket limit $4620; paid at 100% after limit reached	Out-of-pocket limit $2310; paid at 100% after limit reached		

Basic Benefits:

Hospitalization: Part A coinsurance plus coverage for 365 additional days after Medicare benefits end

Medical Expenses: Part B coinsurance (generally 20% of Medicare-approved expenses) or copayments for hospital outpatient services. Plans K, L, and N require insureds to pay a portion of Part B coinsurance or copayments.

Blood: First three (3) pints of blood each year

Hospice: Part A coinsurance

*Plan F also has an option called a high deductible plan F. This high deductible plan pays the same benefits as Plan F after one has paid a calendar year ($2000) deductible. Benefits from high deductible plan F will not begin until out-of-pocket expenses exceed $2000. Out-of-pocket expenses for this deductible are expenses that would ordinarily be paid by the policy. These expenses include the Medicare deductibles for Part A and Part B, but do not include the plan's separate foreign travel emergency deductible.

Benefit Chart of Medicare Supplement Plans
(Source: Connecticut Insurance Department)

Monthly Medicare Supplement rates for Standardized Plans

NOTE: The rates shown may vary by mode of payment. Check with the company for more information.

Company/Individual Plans	A (1)	B (1)	C (1)	D	F	F (2) High Deductible	G	K	L	M	N	Date (3) Approved
American Progressive Life & Health Ins. Company	$284.13	$367.80	$443.05	$402.37	$420.72	$75.58	$369.35				$154.19	11/30/2010
Anthem Blue Cross & Blue Shield	$169.57				$233.73	$39.18	$221.94				$160.65	10/14/2010
Colonial Penn Life Insurance Company	$526.93	$609.65			$404.28	$60.68	$388.43	$129.57	$234.63		$249.09	08/10/2011
Equitable Life & Casualty Insurance Company	$171.17				$253.08					$347.74	$182.25	06/17/2011
Globe Life & Accident Insurance Company	$134.00	$181.00	$209.00		$210.50							02/18/2011
Gov't Personnel Mutual Life Insurance Company	$238.30		$320.72		$246.39		$203.01				$180.18	07/25/2011
Humana Insurance Company	$190.40				$225.12	$88.48	$215.04	$113.12	$163.52			04/09/2010
Pennsylvania Life Insurance Company	$246.00			$265.00	$308.00		$255.00					09/22/2011
State Farm Mutual Automobile Insurance Company	$326.23		$452.63		$350.97							08/22/2011
United American Insurance Company	$177.00	$270.00	$314.00	$309.00	$308.00	$68.00	$303.00	$131.00	$183.00		$189.00	12/30/2010
United of Omaha Life Insurance Company	$357.89		$211.39	$197.60	$255.65		$237.24					03/11/2011
USAA Life Insurance Company	$264.01				$255.68							01/21/2011
Group Plans (4)												
United HealthCare Insurance Company/AARP	$122.75	$178.75	$235.25		$214.50			$78.75	$112.25		$152.75	09/16/2011

(1) Plans for Disabled - All companies must offer Plans A. If a company also offers Plan(s) B and/or C, then it must also offer the plan(s) to disabled Medicare beneficiaries.

(2) High Deductible Plan - This plan provides the same benefits as Plan F after one has paid a calendar year deductible of **$2,000 for 2011**. Out of pocket expenses for this deductible are expenses that would ordinarily be paid by the plan. These expenses include the Medicare A and B expenses that would ordinarily be paid by the plan. These expenses include the Medicare A and B deductibles, but not the foreign travel emergency deductibles.

(3) The date a company's rate was approved is not necessarily the date the rate change will take effect. Check with the company for the effective date.

(4) These are group plans that are available to individuals enrolled in Medicare. Payment of a group membership fee is required.

Monthly Medicare Supplement Rates
(Source: Connecticut Insurance Department)

RESOURCES

There are many resources—local, state and national—that provide assistance to consumers who need information about health or healthcare coverage matters. They include:

* Info-line for information on local resources
* Your community's Area on Aging local agency (to find see www.aoa.gov, or call 800 677-1116 for information on local service for older Americans)
* Local hospitals
* State Insurance Department
* State Medical Society
* State Patient Advocacy or Attorney General's Offices
* Disease Specific Support Groups such as the Cancer Society, Leukemia Society, etc.
* Insurance company, association and Medicare websites, www.medicare.gov
* The Veterans Administration, www1.va.gov/health
* National Patient Advocate Foundation, www.npaf,org, 202 347-8009

Also, anyone looking for information should conduct an internet search on specific topics to determine if other resources might be available.

MAURA LOUGHLIN CARLEY is President and CEO of Healthcare Navigation LLC, a leading healthcare advocacy and consulting firm.

She founded Healthcare Navigation, LLC in 1999, as a result of a passionate belief that consumers and patients deserve professional guidance in dealing with an increasingly complex and adversarial healthcare world. Her company is known for fabulously talented colleagues and staff. It does not sell insurance.

Carley started her healthcare career by chance. As a college student in San Francisco, she provided clerical support to Wanda Jones and the Healthcare Organization and Management Group, a consulting firm. As a graduate student at Yale, she returned to the HOM Group one summer as an administrative resident.

She studied Public Health and Hospital Administration at Yale University and received a Masters in Public Health in 1978. Her professional career began at Yale-New Haven Hospital where she gained first-hand knowledge about the special issues of university teaching hospitals.

Later she accepted a position at Stamford Hospital, a community teaching hospital where she had line responsibility for many hospital departments, worked with outstanding people, and learned how hospitals operate.

Carley made a major career change in the late 1980s and gained experience on the insurance side of the healthcare business, first with a Blue Cross Blue Shield-owned staff model Health Maintenance Organization and later with Kaiser Permanente, one of the oldest and largest group model Health

Maintenance Organizations. These organizations are both providers and insurers of healthcare services.

When Kaiser moved her job to a new geographic location, she chose the "package" instead (and faced her own coverage transition). Before starting Healthcare Navigation, she worked as an executive with a physician practice management company in New York. In that position, a large medical billing department reported up to her and she had a very intensive introduction to the world of diagnostic and procedural coding, insurance exclusions, the complexity of medical billing and the many things that can go wrong so that a claim is not paid.

Carley has worked on "every side of the fence." She understands the pressure that doctors and hospitals are under to maximize revenue and the pressure on insurers. While at Kaiser Permanente, she vividly remembers representatives of large employer groups insisting on "no premium increases" which meant redoubling efforts to reduce hospital and other expenses. For now she prefers advocating on behalf of clients.

She is a fellow in the American College of Healthcare Executives and a Certified Insurance Consultant.

"I am extremely fortunate to have had a diverse healthcare career at executive levels and also blessed by having worked with informed, dedicated people. You know who you are and I thank you all.

I've had the opportunity to speak on healthcare topics at programs across the United States and Canada including television and radio appearances, national webinar broadcasts, conferences, and meetings.

Most important, we have helped clients across the United States and some outside the United States. Our experiences with our clients enabled me to write this book. I thank them all."